WA

FROM THE VILLAGES OF

SNOWDONIA

Hilary Kendell
B.A.

Hilary Bradnam
B.Sc.

**Beddgelert Betws-y-coed
Capel Curig Dolwyddelan
Llanberis Llanrwst Trefriw**

First Edition: August 1987
Second Edition: October 1989
Third Edition: May 1993
Fourth Edition: May 1999
Fifth Edition: April 2008

Published by Hilary Books
ISBN: 978 0-9533315-3-6

ACKNOWLEDGEMENTS:

We would like to thank all those who have helped us in the
preparation of this booklet especially Joshua Bradnam-Smith,
the Howarth family, the Kendell family, Irene Palmer,
Lorna Shipp, Martin Smith, Hazel Wright and the
Whittingham family.

Since printing the 2nd edition, Hilary Kendell
has died after a long illness. It was her wish that
I should continue to publish the books so that more
people may enjoy walking in Snowdonia.

Hilary Bradnam

Printed by
Gwasg Carreg Gwalch, 12 Iard yr Orsaf,
Llanrwst, Dyffryn Conwy.

Enquiries regarding sales:
Hilary Books,
Betws-y-coed

Tel: 01690 710741
E-mail: hilarybooks@aol.com

WALKS FROM THE VILLAGES OF SNOWDONIA

Contents

Introduction

There are many good books which describe the routes by which you can climb to the mountain summits.

This is not one of them.

What you will find in this pocket-sized book are directions to walks which explore the hill slopes and valleys of this beautiful region and lead you to some of the finest viewpoints of the mountain peaks.

They are all-weather walks, possible in all but the very worst of weathers; possible when the mountains are shrouded in mist or white with snow.

They are all circular walks from the villages in the heart of Snowdonia: Beddgelert, Betws-y-coed, Capel Curig, Dolwyddelan, Llanberis, Llanrwst and Trefriw. Some villages, like Beddgelert and Betws-y-coed have been popular as walking centres since Victorian times, but others like Dolwyddelan deserve more attention. Each village has a distinct character influenced partly by its site and the circumstances of its past growth. They all lie reasonably close together and it is quite feasible to choose a walk from each of them during a week's holiday.

All the maps are on the same scale and are sufficiently clear to use without an accompanying map. The distances given within the text are approximate, shorter distances being given in metres only.

The walks have been chosen with families in mind. **Where it is advisable to go ahead of children e.g. on the approach to a waterfall or an unavoidable road crossing, you will find an !** In the countryside there are many natural hazards, so please do not assume that the sign ! marks every steep slope, deep pool etc.

Stout shoes or boots are advised for most of the walks as all tracks may have muddy sections.

Remember the countryside code. Some warnings: avoid areas where forestry work is taking place for operators of machinery cannot hear you. No vehicles are allowed on Forest Enterprise roads without permission; old mines and quarries are dangerous. Dogs are unpopular in most places, especially in the lambing season, so please keep them under close control.

Routes have been chosen to follow public rights of way or routes where use is permitted due to the goodwill of the landowner, but please do not use this book alone as justification for access.

This is a Welsh speaking area and Welsh place-names are used where they are in general use. The following words are interchangeable in the text.

Mountain/Moel;   River/Afon;   Lake/Llyn;
Valley/Nant;   Bridge/Pont or Bont.

Since writing our first book we have realized what a changing countryside it is. If we mentioned a ruined cottage, it was renovated; trees were felled, signs changed. We have tried to avoid giving directions relying on impermanent features, but more features are impermanent than we realized.

While every care has been taken in the preparation of this book, no responsibility can be accepted by the authors.

The area is so rich in history, legends and good stories that it has been difficult trying to select the information. Equally the physical background, the geology and landforms, the flora and fauna are so interesting that a pocket book could easily have expanded into a tome.

Some walks are such obvious choices e.g. the walk around Llyn Crafnant that they have been described elsewhere. We hope that others may be new to you and that you enjoy discovering new ground and new views.

Thank you for your compliments on the earlier editions. In this new edition, all the routes have been walked and re-checked thoroughly, with the instructions updated as necessary.

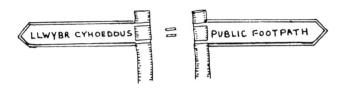

Key to the Maps

——	Tarmac road
======	Track
- - - - -	Path
—•—▪	Railway line with station
→	Route
～	Stream or river
⬤	Lake
▪	Building
▫	Ruin
⚑	Church or Chapel
P	Parking
⠐⠂	Mine or Quarry area
♠	Coniferous forest
♀ ♀	Broad-leafed woodland
※	Viewpoint
km	Kilometre
✳	Place of interest
◯	Village

Location of the Villages

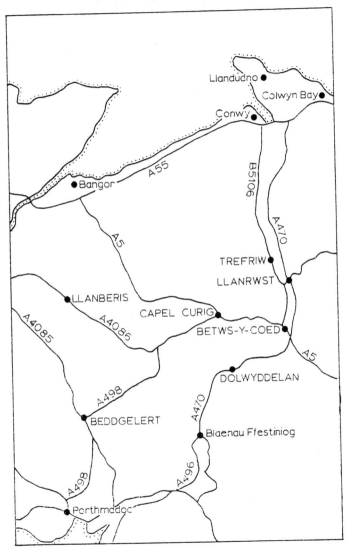

Beddgelert

Beddgelert nestles below the mountains at the junction of the valleys of Nant Gwynant and Afon Glaslyn close to the Aberglaslyn Gorge. It has been a popular spot for tourists since Victorian times and offers a choice of places for accommodation and refreshments. The village has become famous for its popular legend about Prince Llywelyn and his wolfhound, Gelert, but in fact originally grew up as an early Christian site. There is a large car park near to the Royal Goat Hotel in this good walking centre.

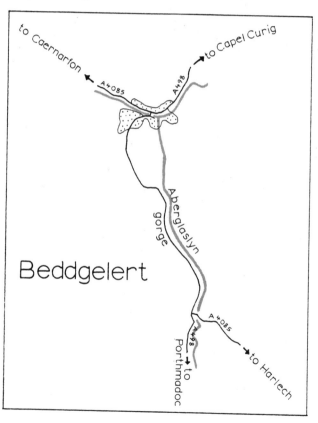

Gelert's Grave Walk

This is a short pleasant walk by the Afon Glaslyn following easy tracks to Gelert's Grave.

For map, see page 11   Distance: 1.5 km / 1 mile

GELERTS GRAVE

DIRECTIONS: The path is signposted from the bridge over the River Glaslyn in the centre of Beddgelert. A short road between the bridge and Llywelyn's Cottage (National Trust) leads beside the river. There are W.C.'s to your right on the way. Do not cross the metal bridge over the confluence of the Afon Colwyn with the Afon Glaslyn but turn right through a metal gate to follow a concrete path by the side of the tree-lined Afon Glaslyn.

On the right is the parish church of St Mary's. The wall (with the narrow windows) which faces the river is part of the 13th century Augustinian Priory which was on

the same site. There was an even earlier 7th century monastery here, said to have been, with Bardsey, the oldest in Wales, which offered hospitality to weary travellers through the region.

Where an old wall meets the path, turn right along another concrete path and through a gate leading to Gelert's Grave which lies in a peaceful pasture in an amphitheatre of hills.

Here on the slate slab resting above the grave you can read the story of Gelert, the faithful dog, mistakenly killed by his master Llywelyn who thought the dog had killed the boy prince. Too late, Llywelyn discovered a dead wolf and the child unharmed.

It is said that the legend was invented by David Pritchard, landlord of the Goat Inn, to boost tourism, but it is too good a story to disbelieve! However the name Beddgelert, grave of Gelert, almost certainly refers to the Celtic Saint Kelert who founded a church here in the 6th century.

Return by the same route.

Aberglaslyn Gorge and Llyn Dinas Walk

Rivers, gorges, valleys, streams, a lake, a railway and a mine. All these can be found on this circular walk, which begins along the Aberglaslyn Gorge, rises over a saddle of moorland before dropping down to Llyn Dinas. It passes old copper mine workings in Cwm Bychan as well as Sygun Mine, where it is possible to go underground. The old fishermen's path is rough and has some steep drops into the river, but is only impassable at times of flood.

For map, see page 11   Distance: 9 km / 5½ miles

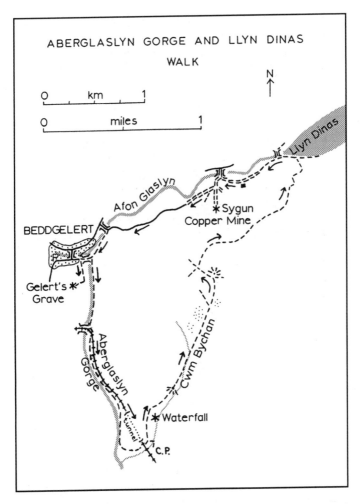

ABERGLASLYN GORGE AND LLYN DINAS
WALK

Llyn Dinas

Afon Glaslyn

Sygun
Copper Mine

BEDDGELERT

Gelert's ✱
Grave

Aberglaslyn
Gorge

Cwm Bychan

Tunnel

✱ Waterfall

C.P.

DIRECTIONS: Turn left from the car park and follow the road as far as the bridge. From here continue straight on alongside the river signposted to Gelert's Grave. Cross the river by the footbridge and turn immediately right to follow the path along the river bank. Continue ahead through two gates to follow the

ABERGLASLYN GORGE

river for 800 metres. ! Where a second footbridge and railway line cross the river, bear left to cross the railway line at a level crossing. Turn left to follow the path between railway and river.

Follow this path as it enters the dramatic Aberglaslyn Gorge, the river water being unusually blue due to its high copper content. The path becomes progressively rougher and rockier and can be slippery. It enters native woodland before reaching a road. Do not go through the kissing gate, but turn left up the steps and continue through a wooden gate in the stone wall ahead. Turn right down towards the car park, then cross the stile to continue ahead under the railway line. Cross the grassy area to pick up the steps rising slightly to the left. Bear right to rejoin the original clear footpath uphill. After about 250 metres, at a small waterfall, go through the gate and continue uphill, with the stream to your right.

The flat valley below is the reclaimed estuary of Afon Glaslyn, in total 1500 acres. Originally this was a beautiful tidal area, but in 1814 William Madocks completed an embankment across the mouth of the estuary and the land behind was reclaimed from the sea. It has, however, always remained poor pasture and even William Madocks' wife complained that the view from their house was more attractive before the developments!

The valley narrows as the path crosses the stream then goes through a gap in the wall to your right by some old sheep enclosures. Just beyond this is the main area of mine workings.

Copper mining began here in Cwm Bychan in the 16th century and continued for over 200 years. Towards the end of this period the ore was transported to the Amlwch smelter on Anglesey. ! Do not enter any of the mine entrances. Here you can see the remains of the cable system. This transported the full trucks of copper downhill by gravity, to be taken away by train, and simultaneously pulled up the empty trucks from the bottom.

Keep straight on, ignoring the path forking left about 75 metres beyond the top of the cable, and head towards the dip in the skyline. At the brow of the hill you get a glimpse of Llyn Dinas way below and the stony path now goes downhill into a heather-clad valley. Cross the stile at the brow of the hill and turn left along the stony path towards some rocky knolls. At the crossroads, with an incongruous signpost, turn right to Llyn Dinas.

Llyn Dinas soon comes clearly into view with the massive Snowdon block ahead and Cnicht on the skyline to your right. The path appears to plunge into the lake but in fact goes down the hillside in easy stages. Keep to the main path which leads to the near end of the lake. At the water's edge turn left along to the river, then turn left again through a kissing gate and follow the river on the near bank. This path is very clear but makes a few detours from the river around field boundaries.

On the summit of the steep afforested slope on the other side of the river lies Dinas Emrys, an Iron Age hill fort, although little remains of the original structure. Welsh legend describes how Vortigern, Welsh born but antagonistic to his fellow men, encouraged Saxon invasions in the area. He attempted to build a castle at Dinas Emrys but the magical powers of Myrddin Emrys removed the foundations each night. (Myrddin Emrys is the same Merlin of the Arthurian legends.) Later Myrddin Emrys himself dwelt at a fortress on Dinas Emrys to which he gave his name.

Follow the signed path, through two gates, passing to the right of the house. Beyond the second gate, the path joins a road. Turn left along it, ignoring the car park on your left and bear right, with the fence on your left, rather than entering the Sygun Mine.

Carry straight on along the road, ignoring the signposted path to Cwm Bychan. Follow it for 1 kilometre to where the road swings right over the river. Here, cross the slate and wood stile ahead to continue along the riverside for about 300 metres, passing two more gates and one road. You are now on the outskirts of Beddgelert. Pass the two rows of cottages on your left around the village green and cross the metal footbridge over the river to arrive back at your starting point.

A Walk above Beddgelert

The views obtained on this walk should not be missed; they are spectacular in all directions. Many of the rhododendrons seen on this walk were planted specially for the film 'Inn of the 6th Happiness'. The path rises to about 900 feet over moorland which can be boggy after rain and the return is along the dramatic Aberglaslyn Gorge. The path is rather indistinct in the middle section from Cwm Cloch farm to Aberglaslyn Hall and for this reason the longer loop should be attempted only by more experienced walkers. Choose a clear day for this walk.

Distance: Shorter loop: 2 km / 1½ miles

For map, see page 16   Longer loop: 6.5 km / 4 miles

DIRECTIONS: **Beddgelert to Aberglaslyn Hall**: From the top of the car park adjacent to the Royal Goat Hotel, go through the wooden gate. Turn left and then sharp right, ignoring both the steps up to the station and the path joining from the left. Through the next gate, turn left under the railway line and immediately right.

This was the old line from Porthmadog to Caernarfon. At the time of going to print, the Welsh Highland Railway is being restored as a tourist attraction.

After 10 metres turn left through a gate and turn right to follow round the edge of the field. Go through the gate, cross the stream and join the track, turning left along it. This track crosses the railway line, passes the farm of Cwm Cloch Isaf and then enters a small pine

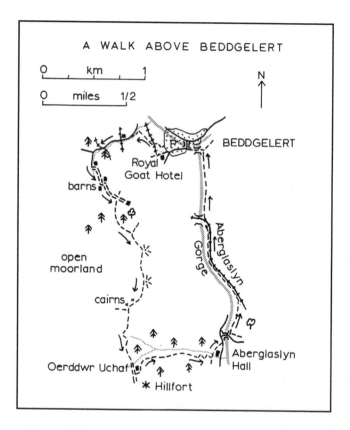

A WALK ABOVE BEDDGELERT

plantation within which another line of the railway is crossed. Continue for 200 metres to Cwm Cloch Canol beyond which the gravel track turns left over a stream and winds across the slope passing between two farm buildings.

> *Nant Gwynant appears on your left with Moel Siabod at its head and Snowdon to the left. Moel Hebog towers on the right of the track with the volcanic-looking Cnicht on the skyline ahead.*

300 metres beyond the buildings, and just before the second patch of trees, gates lead into the fields on either side of the track.

[**Shorter loop**: Turn **left** through the gate. Walk down the slope on this clear footpath, bearing right at the railway line, to bring you back to the Royal Goat Hotel.]

For the longer loop, turn **right** through the signed gate and go straight up the hill keeping the trees away to your left. A walking man sign directs you across an old ditch by a sluice gate from where the path heads upwards towards the fence on your left.

Continue up the slope and go through the padlocked gate in the top corner of the field with the trees to your left. 5 metres beyond the gate bear **right** up the hillside, initially keeping the next patch of trees to your right. The path climbs diagonally up the hill becoming less distinct.

You pass a hut circle as you climb. A 'desirable residence with outstanding views' in prehistoric times. You will see others 'en route'.

When you reach a low ruined stone wall contouring round the slope, turn left to follow it for about 125 metres to reach an obvious gap.

17

Go through the gap to follow a fairly clear path climbing diagonally up the slope, skirting below a rocky outcrop.

> *The full panoramic view can best be appreciated at this point. Beddgelert lies in the valley 800 feet below with Yr Wyddfa (the summit of Snowdon) above it. Looking ahead, adjacent to the conical shaped Cnicht, you see the twin mountains of Moelwyn Mawr and Moelwyn Bach.*

As you continue to climb the slope and approach the top of the spur keep to the **right** of a second rocky outcrop.

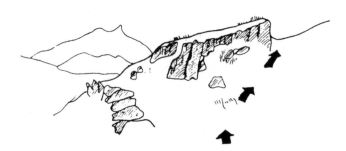

Beyond it the path rises up the slope and bears right. A hollow with two solitary trees and a well built sheep pen lie below to your left. Take the right, narrower, uphill fork at the broken wall, then bear left around the top of the hollow. Climb diagonally around the hillside, following a track which is clearly embanked in some places but indistinct over short stretches, until you reach a wall. Passing through a gap in the wall continue ahead for 75 metres to a white capped cairn. Bear left, slightly downhill, to pass two more cairns capped with quartzite until a wide valley comes into view. Beyond this third cairn turn left beside a rocky outcrop to leave the stony path and descend sharply into the valley.

Pass through a gap in the wall and turn left although there is no clear path. Head towards the obvious circular stone enclosure. Pass to the left of the enclosure and head for a gap between rocky outcrops.

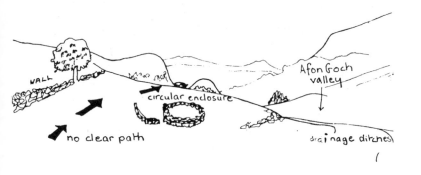

Where the stream enters this rocky cleft, ford it. There are several footpaths crossing the next section, all indistinct in places. The public right of way continues straight ahead along a boggy path on the edge of the flat area with the tops of the crags to your left. After 75 metres, start to drop diagonally down between crags, heading generally in the direction of the largest coniferous tree. Pass through a gap in a broken wall and continue down to reach a wall ending at the largest crag.

Bear left, with the wall on your right, as far as the distinctive iron hoop in the wall. Bear left across a very boggy patch to pick up the wall reappearing out of the bog. Keep this wall on your right for 20 metres, before passing through a gap and following the clear path, with the wall now on your left, down to Oerddwr Uchaf. Pass behind the farm, then immediately turn left through their garden gate.

A slate plaque, dedicated to a local poet, reads:

Yn y Ffermdy hwn	**In this farmhouse**
y ganed ac y maged	**William Francis Hughes**
William Francis Hughes	**"William Oerddwr"**
"William Oerddwr"	**was born and died here**
1879 - 1966	**1879 - 1966**

To the right of the farm is a small round-topped hill encircled by a wall. This is Pen-y-gaer, an Iron Age hill fort. Little of the original fortifications remains as the walls have been built from the original defences.

From Oerddwr Uchaf you descend the steep valley side, following a stream for most of the way. Turn right through a gateway to reach the stream. Bear right down the slope to follow it. After descending a steep rocky section with rhododendrons on your left, bear right heading between the conifer plantation and a little hillock. Leave the second rocky knoll to your right and pass through a gap in the wall ahead. Bear left to leave the sheep enclosure on your right. Further down the slope bear left again to follow a short stone path to rejoin the stream just before it enters a small rhododendron clad ravine. Keep to the edge of this gorge as you follow the path down the steep slope, crossing some patches of rocky ground.

Cross a stile to enter forest, following a mossy, walled track down the hillside. At a private gate turn left, and continue down the slope. Cross the Afon Goch via a footbridge. Bear right, with a fence on your left, past Aberglaslyn Hall, to meet the road.

Aberglaslyn Hall to Beddgelert: ! Turn left along the road to a junction 120 metres away (there is a sharp bend and no pavement) and turn right over Pont Aberglaslyn. Take the gate immediately over the bridge, then take the stepped path along the river bank rather than climbing the steps up to your right.

This old restored fishermen's path is rough and has steep drops into the river in places, but is only impassable in times of flood. Follow it along the river bank of the Aberglaslyn Gorge, crossing the Welsh Highland Railway at a level crossing. Once over the crossing, turn right along the concrete path back towards Beddgelert.

At a gate, on the opposite side of the river, is a Water Authority Gauging Station where the volume of water in the river is monitored regularly. The overhead cable is used for winching out instruments for measuring depth and velocity of the river.

Continue to the village green at the confluence of the two rivers. Turn left over the footbridge, and continue to the main road which leads back to the car park.

Betws-y-coed

Betws-y-coed has a lovely setting at the junction of the three turbulent rivers – Afon Conwy, Afon Lledr and Afon Llugwy. It developed as a Victorian resort and artists' centre. There are plenty of places to visit including the 14th century church by the river, the visitors' centre, motor museum, art gallery, railway museum and good shops. It is a place to wander by the river, but it is also a good walking centre. Four walks are described here, more can be found in 'WALKS AROUND BETWS-Y-COED'. Close by are the familiar beauty spots of Fairy Glen and Swallow Falls. There is plenty of parking both on and off the road.

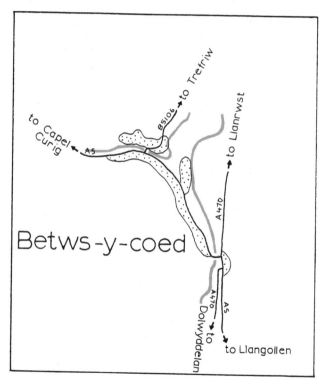

Artists' Wood Walk

This is a beautiful walk alongside Afon Llugwy, returning through beech woodlands. It is so named after the many Victorian artists who frequented the area, inspired by the outstanding scenery. There are no steep sections on this walk. This path can be flooded after heavy rain.

Distance: 5.5 km / 3½ miles

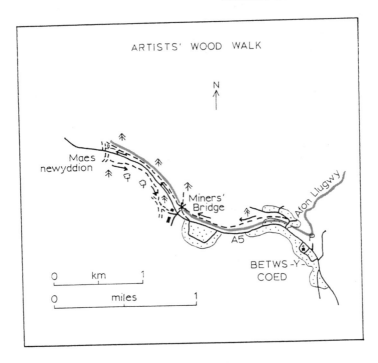

ARTISTS' WOOD WALK

N

Maes newyddion

Miners' Bridge

A5

Afon Llugwy

BETWS-Y-COED

0   km   1

0   miles   1

DIRECTIONS: From the A5 cross Pont-y-Pair, the stone bridge signposted to Trefriw. Immediately turn left, passing the car park, and immediately left again onto the footpath between the river and the all-ability path. Follow it through the woods along the river bank and enter the field by a stile. Cross this field, again keeping to the edge of the river, and after crossing a second stile the path re-enters woodland. The river banks become progressively steeper until you reach Miners' Bridge.

MINERS BRIDGE

Miners' Bridge was built originally to provide a short-cut for miners living in Pentre-du who worked in the lead mines on the plateau to the north of the village. All the mines are closed now, but during the 19th century they provided considerable employment in the area. It is close to the place where the Romans used to cross Afon Llugwy on the Sarn Helen route way.

Cross the bridge, climb the steps, and immediately turn right along the path. Follow the path through the trees adjacent to Afon Llugwy. Along this stretch there are numerous places where it is possible to walk down to the river. After a few hundred metres the path veers away from the river rising over a bluff. After a further few hundred metres, take the left hand fork, and cross a stream by a footbridge. Continue to some derelict lead mine buildings, the mine entrance being visible on the opposite bank with the remains of the tramway supports. Turn left up to the main road, and then left along the pavement for 30 metres. ! Cross the road.

Return route: Walk up the forest track signed Maes Newyddion and after 20 metres turn left along the narrow path. After 75 metres bear left through dense conifers and drop down past some boulders. The route continues above the A5 over a wooden footbridge and through beech trees. Pass to the left of the Forestry Commission commemorative stone, cross two more footbridges and take the left fork. Continue through the woodland which becomes coniferous shortly before joining a track. Turn left on this track and follow the road down to the A5. Here you can return to Betws-y-coed by turning right along the main road, or by crossing straight over, past the wooden barrier down to Miners' Bridge and returning as for the outward journey.

> *Probably the best-known of the many artists who were attracted to Betws-y-coed in the 19th century are J.M.W. Turner and David Cox. The latter came to stay here each summer from 1844 to 1856 staying mostly with the Roberts at the newly built Royal Oak Hotel. The sign board he painted for the Royal Oak (oil on wood) can be seen hanging above the fireplace in the reception area. It shows Charles II very well hidden in an oak tree at Boscobel.*

The Llyn Elsi and Hafod-las Walk

This upland walk incorporates forest, woodland and farmland; it passes **Llyn Elsi** with spectacular views of the mountains, and crosses the old slate quarry of **Hafod-las**. It returns on **Sarn Helen**, a Roman road. The first part is steep, but once the lake has been reached the walk is almost flat or downhill. It is possible to extend the walk round the lake.

Distance: 5.5 km / 3½ miles

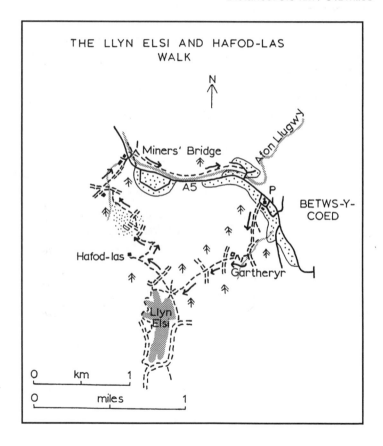

THE LLYN ELSI AND HAFOD-LAS WALK

N

Miners' Bridge

Afon Llugwy

A5

P

BETWS-Y-COED

Hafod-las

Gartheryr

Llyn Elsi

0   km   1

0   miles   1

DIRECTIONS: From the A5 take either road uphill beside St Mary's Church and turn up the track to the right of the modern bungalow. After about 600 metres, at a standing stone, turn right on a well-defined path which crosses the stream by a wooden bridge. This path zigzags up the steep slope to the top of the crags. At the top, the path flattens and passes a ruined cottage called Gartheryr on your right.

In 1749 a Calvinistic Methodist came to live in Betws-y-coed and weekly meetings were held in Gartheryr. The congregations grew to such a size that famous Welsh preachers came to visit the cottage.

Continue along the gentler path, crossing straight over at two tracks. At the top of the rise, Llyn Elsi comes into view. Continue on to the monument.

At this point you can see many of the mountains of Snowdonia (but not Snowdon!). Straight ahead is Moel Siabod; the next upland area includes the Glyders and Tryfan (three peaks), and finally the right-hand ridge comprises the Carneddau.

[DETOUR: **Round the lake:** Take the path heading steeply downhill towards the lake. Continue on a mixture of tracks and paths, always taking the right hand route. N.B. Look out for the steep path downhill leading from the track halfway along the western side, marked by some rocks. After climbing concrete steps and dropping down to a bridge, continue straight ahead with the dam to your right to return to the monument.]

With your back to the inscription, take the gravel path to your left downhill. After 80 metres, where the path veers left, carry straight on through birch trees on a muddy path to a track. Turn left, past the barrier, and after 20 metres turn right. Continue along this path, then cross a fence by the stile so there is now a wall to your right and a fence to your left. Continue along the path until, shortly before Hafod-las Cottage, a grassy track doubles back to the right, adjacent to some old machinery. Turn right along the track with a wall on your left. Continue down this winding track until you reach the barn. Here turn sharp left along the track with a fence on your right.

Enter the woodland and Hafod-las slate quarry by a stile. Follow the wire fence on your left until the track turns sharp right. Here there is a view into the overgrown quarry.

Continue on the track downhill. Immediately after the wall on your right becomes a fence, turn left along the level path which leads towards the quarry buildings. ! Do not enter any ruins or clamber on the spoil heaps.

> *Hafod-las quarry is a small slate quarry which was operative mainly in the 19th century. The quarry workers lived in Pentre-du, directly below, or in Rhiwddolion, an isolated and now almost deserted village on Sarn Helen, the Roman Road.*

Walk along the old tramway to the gate. Just before the gate turn right down a narrow path. This path leads steeply downhill to the right, partly hidden by tree branches, to a small stream. Cross the stream and continue past two small ruined buildings.

> *There are spoil heaps on either side; notice the difference in the stones comprising them. On your right are huge blocks from the initial quarrying whereas on your left are split slates which are reject roofing tiles.*

Keep close to the right of the second building as the path drops down to an old inclined tramway. After 10 metres, turn left over the stile into the field.

Cross the field keeping the base of the spoil heaps to your left. Continue to the far end where there is a stile leading into woodland. Cross the stile and follow the narrow path through the many fallen trees towards a stream, then follow the path down to a track. Turn left and walk along the track for 150 metres to crossroads.

Turn right down the path, crossing a bridge, a stile, then a gate and continue down to the main road. Here you have the choice of following the road or the riverbank. For the former, turn right down the A5. For the latter walk, cross straight over, pass the wooden barrier and follow the path down to Afon Llugwy. Cross Miners' Bridge and turn right along the river bank back to Betws-y-coed.

The Conwy Gorge, Fairy Glen, Conwy Falls and the Machno Falls

This is a walk following one of the loveliest stretches of water in the district as Afon Conwy falls over a series of rapids and waterfalls to the pool below Beaver Bridge. There are no steep hills to climb on this easy circuit. Allow plenty of time to explore **Fairy Glen**, see the **Conwy Falls, Machno Falls** and **Roman Bridge**. The Conwy gorge remains virtually unchanged since its popularity in Victorian times and is very un-commercialized although a small charge is made to see the Conwy Falls and Fairy Glen. It is possible to shorten this walk by parking at Fairy Glen.

For map, see page 30   Distance: 11 km / 7 miles

DIRECTIONS: **To Fairy Glen**: Follow the A5 downhill from Pont-y-Pair, past the church and Post Office to take the minor road which turns right off the A5, towards Betws Motors. Follow it for 1.5 km / 1 mile through pleasant woodlands to Beaver Bridge. ! Take care where the railway bridge crosses the road.

> *Beaver Pool (Llyn yr Afanc) is a wide welling pool where the Afon Conwy rests after its turbulent journey. It was not always considered a peaceful spot for the Welsh 'afanc' is more likely to refer to an aquatic monster than the likeable and docile beaver. Legends persist of the 'afanc' which was dragged in chains out of this pool by oxen and taken over Moel Siabod to be dropped into the 'bottomless' lake of Llyn-y-ffynnon las.*

! Turn left over Beaver Bridge to cross the busy A470. Immediately turn right between the Fairy Glen Hotel and Beaver Bridge to follow the signed track for 150metres to a gate. Here it is worthwhile making the detour to Fairy Glen. ! The slate steps may be slippery in wet weather.

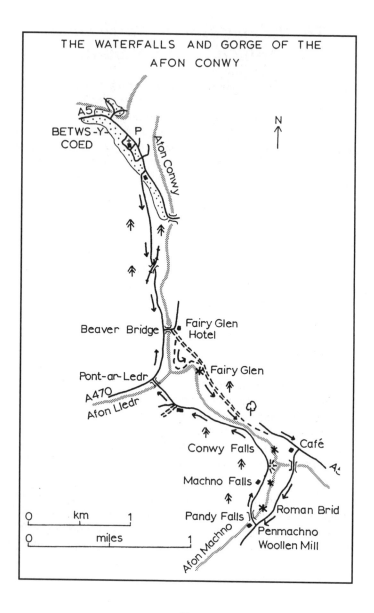

THE WATERFALLS AND GORGE OF THE
AFON CONWY

A5

BETWS-Y-
COED

P

Afon Conwy

N

Beaver Bridge

Fairy Glen
Hotel

Pont-ar-Ledr

Fairy Glen

A470
Afon Lledr

Conwy Falls

Café

A5

Machno Falls

Pandy Falls

Roman Brid

Penmachno
Woollen Mill

km   1

0

miles   1

0

Afon Machno

FAIRY GLEN

Fairy Glen, Ffos Noddyn. A famous 'beauty spot' best seen when shafts of sunlight beam into the deep ravine. The Welsh name Ffos (a ditch) and Noddyn (anoddyn – a chasm) gives a more dramatic impression than the sentimental Victorian name.

The Walk to Conwy Falls: Returning to the track, turn right (through the gate) for 1 km / ¾ mile to reach the A5. At first this is a wide gated track which narrows into a path through woodland as it approaches the A5, muddy when wet.

This track was the old tollgate road on the London to Holyhead route and before that a packhorse trail. The oak trees which are seen on this unspoilt and peaceful walk are the remnants of the extensive oak forests of the upper Conwy Valley. To your right are views over the Lledr Valley towards Moel Siabod and to your left the rocky outcrop of Dinas Mawr.

! Through an opening join the A5. Turn right, taking great care along this busy section of road for 150 metres to the Conwy Falls Café and the entrance to Conwy Falls.

Here the Conwy rushes into an amphitheatre-like hollow of strongly jointed rock. The stream, stained brown by its journey through peat, is divided by a buttress of rock on which you can see the remains of an old salmon ladder which never worked. The new salmon ladder was completed in 1993.

To the Woollen Mill and Roman Bridge: From the A5 turn right to follow the B4406 for 1 km to the crossroads and turn right.

Penmachno Woollen Mill was established in the 1830's as a 'pandy': a fulling mill where cloth woven on the local farms was brought by the farmers to be beaten under the fulling hammers (driven by a water wheel) to matt the fibres. The mill gradually expanded to include carding, spinning and weaving. It remained a family mill until the 1960's but sadly, it is now closed. Next door is an old toll bar.

Pass the mill to cross Afon Machno and Pandy Falls over Pont y Pandy. Look right to see 'Roman Bridge'. This narrow and lovely arch is probably a mediaeval packhorse bridge.

'ROMAN BRIDGE'

THE RETURN JOURNEY: **The Machno Falls:** Continue on the minor road over Pont y Pandy for 500 metres to the Machno Falls. You will find them on the right, marked by a green signpost, immediately opposite Pandy Mill House. (Notice the old potato clamp to the left of the house). Almost hidden from the road, the falls are only a few yards away. ! Take great care as there is no fencing. Little known and un-commercialised, this is the best of the waterfalls!

An old guide book describes the falls as follows: 'Nature has doubly been assisted by art for the old mill wheel plays a most effective part in the view.' Sadly the wheel has gone but the shell of the old corn mill is still standing. The clear water of the Afon Machno is turquoise as it falls into the chasm and surges into the cleft below.

As you continue along the road there are several points at which you can get a view into the gorge. 100 metres from the Machno Falls there is a viewpoint.

The confluence of Afon Machno (on the right) and Afon Conwy (flowing straight towards you) is dramatic below the towering cliffs. After rain, the Afon Conwy waters are coloured a peaty brown in contrast to the turquoise of Afon Machno.

Follow the road downhill for 1 km (ignoring the tracks which join from the left beyond Green Tub Cottage) to Pont ar Ledr. ! Cross the busy A470 and turn right along the stony path adjacent to the road.

To your right, behind the ruin of an old tollgate lies the pool of Llyn Tyn-y-cae where the Lledr joins the Conwy.

Before crossing Beaver Bridge, turn left to follow the minor road for 1.5 km back to Betws-y-coed.

Capel Garmon and the Neolithic Tomb

After an initial climb up the valley side, this is an easy and pleasant walk on a rolling upland plateau to the east of the Conwy, where, unimpeded by trees, you can enjoy wide views of Snowdonia. In a landscape of small farms and in a region of early settlement there is plenty of interest, especially the **Neolithic Burial Chamber** to the south of **Capel Garmon**.

To return, you can choose between A) following the edge of the upland plateau or B) descending into the Conwy Valley to see **Conwy Falls** and returning via **Fairy Glen**.

For map, see page 36   Distance: 10 km / 6 miles

DIRECTIONS: **To Capel Garmon:** From Pont-y-Pair follow the A5 downhill, past the Church and the Post Office, continuing across the Waterloo Bridge to the Ty Gwyn Hotel.

> *The Waterloo Bridge, 'the Iron Bridge', is constructed entirely of cast iron. It was built in 1815 to carry Telford's London to Holyhead road. It is decorated with the national symbols, the rose, the leek and the thistle.*

You will find the path to the left of the Hotel. Steps help you to climb the first part of what is obviously a very old track. Cross a forestry track and continue upwards to where the path narrows before joining a tarmac drive. Turn left along the drive for 50 metres, then turn right through a gap in the wall. Cross a track, climb over a stile and follow the footpath through a copse for 150 metres. Stone steps lead over a stile into a field by a telegraph pole. Follow the left hand boundary stepping over another stile to follow the path uphill. Continue until you reach the track to Gelli Lynnon Farm but do not enter the farmyard. Instead, turn right at a sharp angle up a stony track into a field. The path across the field is not very clear but keeping to the left you will soon see a kissing gate ahead. This is a good spot at which to relax and enjoy the view westwards to the mountains.

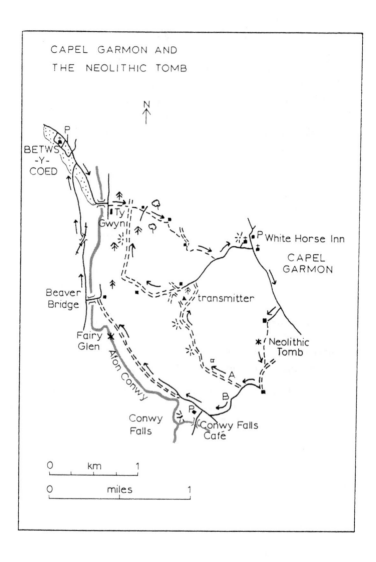

CAPEL GARMON AND
THE NEOLITHIC TOMB

N

BETWS
-Y-
COED

P

Ty
Gwyn

White Horse Inn

P

CAPEL
GARMON

Beaver
Bridge

transmitter

Fairy
Glen

Neolithic
Tomb

Afon Conwy

A

B

Conwy
Falls

P

Conwy Falls
Café

0   km   1

0   miles   1

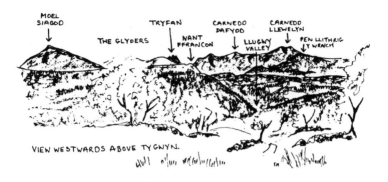

MOEL SIABOD

THE GLYDERS

TRYFAN

NANT FFRANCON

CARNEDD DAFYDD

LLUGWY VALLEY

CARNEDD LLEWELYN

PEN LLITHRIG LY WRACH

VIEW WESTWARDS ABOVE TYGWYN.

Keep the low wall on your left until a wall joins on your right. Continue straight ahead to join a farm track. Turn right and pass through the farm yard at Pant y Pwll. These are kennels, so don't worry about the dogs barking. At the end of the buildings on your right, bear right through a small iron gate to the left of a stone outbuilding. The path now curves to cross a wooded gully. Ignore the first left, but cross the stream over stone slabs and climb upwards to a stepped stile. Cross an area of rough pasture, keeping a wall to your right, and you will soon see the village of Capel Garmon in the distance to your left. The track is muddy as it crosses a stream. A large boulder to the right of an open gateway (and stile) marks the way into the next field. Cross this field heading for the roof of the farm building ahead.

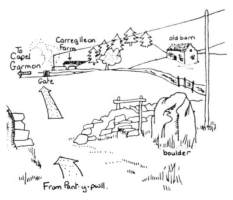

Carreg lleon Farm

old barn

To Capel Garmon

Gate

boulder

From Pant y pwll.

Turn left onto a tarmac track for 500 metres to Capel Garmon. [If you wish you can leave the track at the base of the hill before it reaches the village, turning left over a stepped stile to climb the slope to reach the rear of the church. The view is splendid. Cross the stile to the left of the church wall and follow the path up to the road. Turn right to the chapel.] The tarmac track joins the main road opposite the chapel. Turn left if you wish to walk into the centre of the village to the White Horse Inn or right to continue the walk to the Capel Garmon Neolithic Tomb.

TO THE
WHITE
HORSE
INN

TO THE
NEOLITHIC TOMB

ENTERING CAPEL GARMON

To the Capel Garmon Neolithic Tomb: From the road junction by the chapel turn right to follow the road for 750 metres / ½ mile to a sign marked 'Ystafell Gladdu Capel Garmon Burial Chamber'. Turn right along the track to Tyn Coed which lies in a dell to the right. Where the farm track curves to the right to enter the farmyard, take a signed footpath leading through a gate along the fence to a second gate. You will now see the tomb (surrounded by fencing to protect it from cattle).

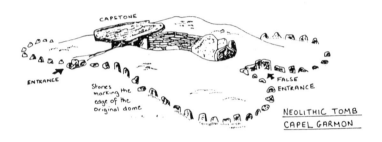

The Capel Garmon tomb was built about 5,000 years ago as a communal burial ground for the local people. (There is another 2 miles to the N.E. of Nebo: 'Maen Pebyll'.) Originally it would have been a smooth, long mound of earth (a long barrow) 94' long and 42' at its widest. Today stones mark the edges of the former mound. Inside all the three chambers would originally have been capped by large stones but only one remains. The tomb has a false entrance; the two horns of the mound gave the impression that the entrance was on the east side, whereas a hidden entrance led from the south. In the middle of the last century it was used as a stable and in 1924 work was done to prevent it deteriorating any further.

To Penrhyddion Farm: On leaving the tomb, turn right to cross the stile, leaving the knoll to your left. Follow the footpath signs which point to the left over an area of rough pasture and through a gap in a wall. Climb up a slight rise and cross a field until you meet a farm track. Turn right along this muddy track towards Penrhyddion Farm.

As you approach the buildings, bear right on a footpath diversion and follow the fence down to the road. Turn right. Follow the road for 200 metres to where it enters rough pasture through a gate.

This is decision time for you can, if you wish, return via the Conwy Valley in which case see page 42 or follow the edge of the upland to rejoin the track to Ty Gwyn.

A. The return route: following the edge of the upland: Turn right onto a muddy track which climbs steadily through an area of rough pasture past the ruins of Tyn-y-gerddi. To your left you look beyond the hump of Dinas Mawr into the Machno and Lledr valleys, while ahead in the west is Moel Siabod.

Bear to the right of a locked gate (see overleaf).

Where the track is seemingly blocked by a locked gate alongside a radio transmitter bear to the right to follow the track which hugs a wall (on your left) bordering forested land. The track leads to a gate opening onto a patch of rough grazing adjoining a tarmac road. Turn left along the road, passing on your right the single storey building of Cefn Rhydd. Bearing right beyond the farm, follow the road for 300 metres to its end.

Beyond Cefn Rhydd.

As you round the bend you will see Tan-y-Bwlch on your left known to local people as the former home of the late gamekeeper 'Bob' whose 'white' horse would bring him back faithfully from the White Horse Inn. Continue along the forestry road (which is barred to vehicles) for 1.5 km / ¾ mile. Ignore the track leading to the right beyond Tan-y-Bwlch and the one which descends the slope to your left as you round the spur. As you near Betws-y-coed, you will have a 'bird's-eye' view in a recently felled area.

Where electricity lines cross the track turn left to follow a steep path bordering a field wall to join the A5 to the right of the Ty Gwyn Hotel. ! Cross the busy A5 and continue over the Waterloo Bridge to Betws-y-coed.

B. The return route via the Conwy Valley: Continue along the track from Penrhyddion Farm past a caravan site to the A5. ! Cross the busy A5 to Conwy Falls Café and the entrance to Conwy Falls (details: page 32). ! Follow the A5 downhill for 150 metres. The road is very busy and there is no footpath. Leave the road at a gap which is the entrance to the old road (replaced by Telford's road in 1815). It is now a path through woodland with views of the Conwy in a deep gorge to the left.

> *George Borrow travelling along the old road in 1862 describes this section. 'At length I came to a steep mountain gorge down which the road ran nearly due north, the Conway to the left running with great noise parallel with the road amongst broken rocks which chaffed it into foam.'*

The path widens to a safe and peaceful track with views over the Lledr Valley towards Moel Siabod to the left and the crags of Dinas Mawr rising to your right.

> *'An immense mountain on the right of the road particularly struck my attention and on enquiring of a man breaking stones by the roadside, I learned that it was called Dinas Mawr or the large citadel perhaps from a fort having been built upon it to defend the pass . . . ' George Borrow, Wild Wales 1854.*

Beyond the fifth gateway is the entrance to Fairy Glen (see page 31).

The track continues down hill to join the A470. To return to the centre of Betws-y-coed turn left over Beaver Bridge and immediately right to follow a minor road following the river to your right. ! Take care where a railway bridge crosses the road. Where this minor road joins the A5, turn left to return you to the centre of the village.

Capel Curig

When you reach the road junction of the A5 with the A4086 and wonder where Capel Curig is, you are there! The small group of buildings is the nucleus of a wide area of scattered homes typical of the dispersed settlement of the area. It has long been a haven for weary travellers, with famous coaching inns such as the former Royal Hotel (now Plas-y-Brenin) and Cobden's. As the nearest village to the mountain core it is a popular centre for mountain activities. There is only limited parking in Capel Curig.

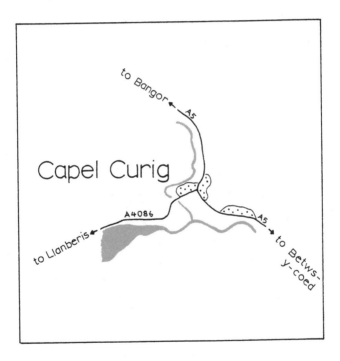

A Walk around Capel Curig

Starting as an easy walk on the valley lowlands, this walk crosses the Afon Llugwy opposite Cobden's Hotel to return on higher ground. From here you can enjoy the classic view of Snowdon reflected in the Llynnau Mymbyr (the twin lakes).

Distance: 5 km / 3 miles

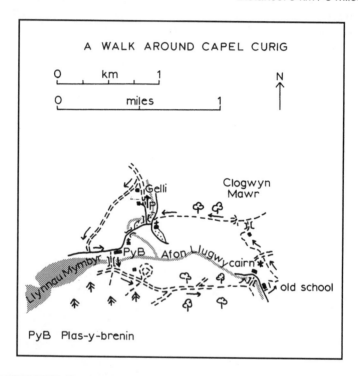

DIRECTIONS: Take the road to the left of the general stores and follow it past Joe Brown's shop and the car park. Continue uphill to carry straight on past Gelli Farm and over the stile, where the road deteriorates to a rough track. Walk 80 metres beyond the ruined barn before turning sharp left to follow an old track.

The track crosses rocks smoothed and scratched by the action of ice. It is difficult to ignore the effects of the Ice Age in the valleys around Capel Curig.

Just before the farm, take the left fork, keeping the fence on your left. The track is well-marked all the way, passing two gates and leading to a stepped stile to join the road. Turn left along the road for 100 metres then turn right over a stile down the signed footpath. This path leads down to the lake adjacent to Plas-y-Brenin, the Outdoor Centre for Mountain Activities.

Plas-y-Brenin was built in 1800 by Thomas Pennant, a Bethesda quarry owner, as the Capel Curig Inn: a hotel with great style. It became so popular with royalty, including Queen Victoria, that it was renamed the Royal Hotel.
If you wish to enquire about joining in the many activities at Plas-y-Brenin which include skiing, canoeing, climbing, and orienteering, telephone Capel Curig 720214.

LOOKING OVER THE LLYNAU MYMBYR TOWARDS SNOWDON

Follow the path down the slope. Cross the footbridge and turn left to follow a gated forestry track for about 500 metres. 50 metres after a track joins on the right, take the right fork to pass a barrier. As the track approaches the river (now the Afon Llugwy) it peters out and steps lead to a path.

! The path climbs the slope to follow the top of the Llugwy gorge. It divides over a rocky knoll and rejoins on the other side bearing left to cross a footbridge opposite Cobden's Hotel.

This was a favourite area for artists in Victorian times. Cobden's Hotel is one of the well-known coaching inns which gave Capel Curig its reputation for hospitality.

Cross the busy A5, and turn right.

Cobden's Hotel to the centre of Capel Curig: From the hotel follow the pavement for 100 metres to the old primary school. Turn left over a stile on the far side of the school to follow a marked footpath (walking man). It follows the school boundary wall before zigzagging up the wooded slope. At a T-junction, turn left and continue up to a stile.

Beyond the stile, continue straight ahead and within a few metres fine views of the mountains can be seen. The path crosses the field keeping to approximately the same height. If you look back to the left you will see the pile of stones which is all that remains of a prehistoric tomb.

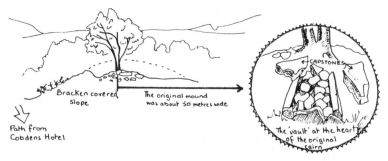

Prehistoric burial site near Cobdens Hotel, Capel Curig

The path crosses a grassy cart-track and continues round the slope through a wall opening to a stile. It rounds a spur keeping to the right of a wooden bungalow. You now face Clogwyn Mawr, a mass of resistant rock formed from volcanic ash, shaped like a gigantic molehill. Follow the fence on your right round the spur to join a track and continue along it. As the track sweeps left, go through the gate straight ahead (to the left of Bryn Tyrch Uchaf gate). Follow the grassy track for 15 metres before turning right to follow a path, crossing a stile as it skirts the garden boundary.

When you reach the house on your right the path crosses boggy ground. Keeping the garden, then a rocky knoll, to your right, walk away from the view over small streams and waterlogged ground for about 50 metres to cross a stone footbridge over the main stream.

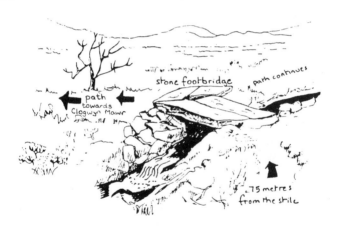

Immediately over the bridge turn left along a rough path heading towards Clogwyn Mawr for about 50 metres to meet a well-defined stony path. Turn left (to a fantastic view!) to follow this old pack-horse trail which winds round the base of Clogwyn Mawr for the next 750 metres, crossing two stiles. Ignore the tracks leading down the slope to the left to join the A5. The walk passes through native oak woodlands before reaching open, often waterlogged ground. Keep the rocks, known as The Pinnacles, to your left and continue for about

200 metres to meet a clearly defined path which descends to the A5 opposite the shops. !! This is a dangerous section of the A5. Cross the road back to the Shop.

A Walk in the Llugwy Valley

A pleasant walk which explores the Llugwy Valley. It has a leisurely start on the valley floor, passing the site of the Roman fort, Caer Llugwy. It returns on higher ground with good views which culminate in a spectacular view of the heartland of Snowdonia. There are only a few uphill sections but some patches of rough ground on the return journey.

The walk can be extended from the 'AROUND CAPEL CURIG WALK' (Map, page 44). At Cobden's Hotel, open to non-residents, parking is possible **IF** you seek permission.

For map, see page 49   Distance: 8 km / 5 miles

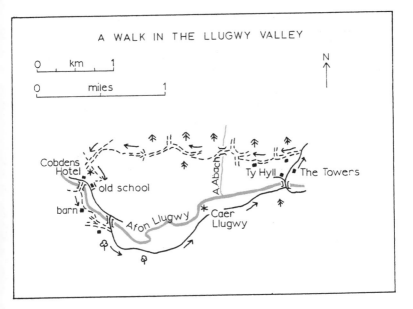

A WALK IN THE LLUGWY VALLEY

Cobdens Hotel

old school

barn

Afon Llugwy

Caer Llugwy

A Abach

Ty Hyll

The Towers

N

DIRECTION: **Cobden's Hotel to Ugly House/Ty Hyll:** Cross the footbridge over Afon Llugwy on the opposite side of the A5 to the hotel. It is possible to turn immediately left but to avoid clambering over rocks you can climb the steps to the 'walking man' sign and turn left down the slope to join the river path. A clamber over the next small rocky outcrop is unavoidable but after that this is a level path bordering Afon Llugwy, a delightful stretch. After crossing a wooden stile continue alongside the river. The path is marked clearly by 'walking man' signs on wooden posts.

Where an overhead wire crosses the path, bear right away from the river towards a house. Cross a stream by a wooden bridge and bear left up a slope to a track. Turn left down the track facing Pont Cyfyng.

Now a quiet bridge over the foaming Llugwy, Pont Cyfyng was a busy crossing at the beginning of the last century for it carried the main road from Capel Curig to Betws-y-coed. Here the coaches carrying passengers

49

and mail between London and Holyhead (and Ireland) crossed the river.

Do not cross the bridge but turn right away from the river to follow a road to follow the valley floor for 3 kilometres.

The old buildings which cluster near the bridge are reminders of the busy slate quarrying community here in the last century. Look for the base of the old tramway which brought the slate down from the quarries on the hillside above. It is almost hidden amongst the trees on the slope past the raised row of cottages on the right.

Roughly halfway along this section of the valley, 1.5 kilometres from Pont Cyfyng, is the site of a Roman fort 'Caer Llugwy'. Look for it on the left after the river approaches the road opposite the entrance to a camping site.

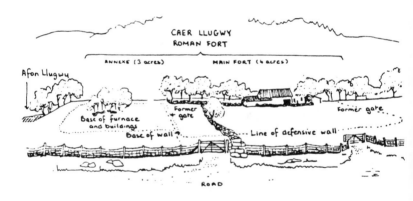

Little remain to show that there was fort here
in A.D. 100 for over 5,000 men.

Little remains today to show that there was an impressive fort here in A.D.100 for over 5,000 men. The defensive walls and ditches measured 45 feet across. The remains of a large furnace may indicate that lead ores, mined to the north, were concentrated here.

The road meets the A5 by the bridge over the Llugwy, Pont Ty Hyll. **!** Cross the busy A5 and bridge to Ty Hyll.

> *Ty Hyll is a supposed result of a loophole in the local laws. It was said that if a house could be built between sunset and sunrise with smoke coming out of the chimney by dawn then the builders owned the house and land.*

From Ty Hyll (Ugly House) to Cobden's Hotel: Take the steep road which leaves the A5 to the right of Ty Hyll. There follows a strenuous uphill climb passing on your right the Towers Outdoor Pursuits Centre. 400 metres from Ty Hyll, turn sharply to the left to follow a forestry track which skirts the woodland edge. After 100 metres, take the track to the left. Follow it for the next kilometre.

There are views of Moel Siabod to the south and on a clear day the Snowdon Horseshoe is visible to the west. It is clearly a very old track bordered in places by substantial walls. The following pointers are useful:

a) where the path forks, 85 metres beyond a bungalow on your left, continue on the path straight ahead, along the field wall.

b) where you cross a fence and ford a stream, the track bears left.

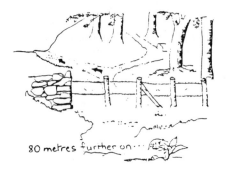

80 metres further on···

The remains of an old lead mine lie below the track in the field before reaching the second bungalow.

c) Beyond a second bungalow on your left, ignore the gated track leading downhill but continue straight ahead over a stile. Ford the stream and follow the path which bears left following the forest edge.

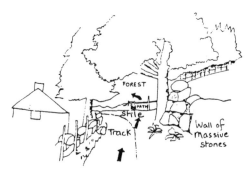

150 metres further on ····

The path continues for 175 metres to join a forestry track. Bear left to follow the track to a junction. Turn right. After only 50 metres, and before reaching a bend in the track, turn left along a path to enter the partly felled forest (see diagram).

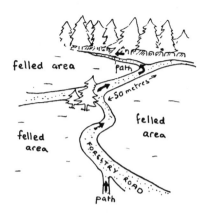

This path is sometimes muddy in places especially before it crosses the Afon Abach by a wooden footbridge, missing at the time of going to print. After crossing the stream and climbing through younger trees, it passes through a newly planted area of conifers before rising to meet a forestry track. Bear left to follow the track over level or gently undulating ground for the next kilometre. Ignore a track leading off to the right. Pass through a turning circle to gain a superb view over the heartland of Snowdonia.

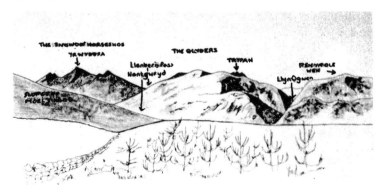

Walk down the slope, facing the mountains, following a grassy track to where the main track swings right. Continue straight ahead to cross two stiles. Join an old track which is clearly visible running down the slope between a wall and a fence. In places the track is very rough, in-filled with stones and rushes and it crosses one small stile.

As the track descends into a small valley partly obscured by bushes, cross a stile and a small stream, then enter an area of scattered trees.

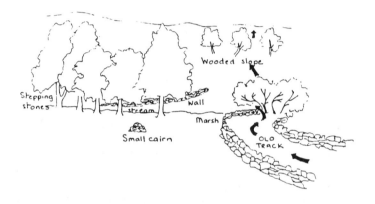

Follow the path diagonally up the slope to cross a broken wall, then a stile. Bear left to follow a path which rises over the brow to reveal good views. Facing you immediately ahead is the hump of Clogwyn Mawr (the large cliff).

The path downhill is indistinct but has marked posts. Descend through rough pasture for about 250 metres facing Clogwyn Mawr. At a crossroads of paths, at the base of the slope, turn left along a narrow track which passes to the left of a tree-clad knoll. The track widens, descending to a stile. About 50 metres down the field, by a gap in the wall on your right, turn **left** to enter a wooded hollow. Over the stile, follow the clear path down the wooded hillside. Cross a stream, then fork right down a clear stony footpath to the A5 below. Turn right to return to Cobden's Hotel.

A Walk to Llyn Crafnant

This is not a circular walk, but because of the most spectacular views en route, it is worthwhile doing a 'there and back'. The route is all on clear paths rising gently over moorland to reach a spectacular viewpoint above Llyn Crafnant. It may be lengthened by combining it with the 'Around Llyn Crafnant' Walk on page 104.

Distance 5.5 km / 3½ miles

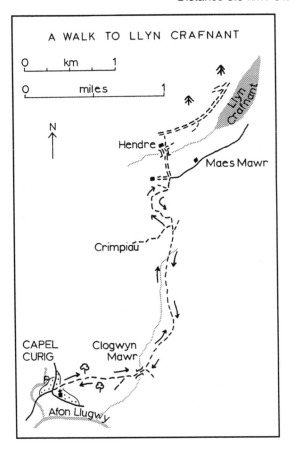

DIRECTIONS: Cross the A5 from the shops and cross the stile to the left of the gate adjacent to the old church. Take the old slabbed path as it rises up the field. Through a gap in the wall continue straight on the stony path ignoring the grassy track leading off to the left.

On your right are the Pinnacles, a distinctive rocky knoll frequented by rock climbers. The old slabs on the path are the remnants of the packhorse trail which followed this route.

This sometimes muddy, but mostly paved, path crosses a boggy area and then enters woodland by a gate and stile. After 400 metres, cross the stile ahead to enter moorland. Continue up the path with a wire fence on your right and pass through a gap in the wall. Here there is an open view of the route ahead.

Cross the oversized footbridge and take the left hand signed path. From here the path is clear, rising gently and curving round the boggy area and stream on your left. After nearly 2 kilometres, as you approach the saddle with Crimpiau to your left, ignore the right hand fork rising uphill.

[DETOUR: To **Crimpiau Summit**. The climb is well-worth the effort as you are rewarded by spectacular views. Take the path on your left near the highest point. There are numerous paths leading up to the summit but beware, some end in sudden steep drops.]

Return by the same route to Capel Curig.

If you wish to extend the walk to Llyn Crafnant, from the saddle continue along the path downhill. This wide stony and grassy path zigzags down the hill, curving round the high crags. After 450 metres it bears right, heading towards the lake. Pass through a gap in the wall ahead, and follow the fence and wall on your left for 80 metres.

Turn left over a stile and take the right fork, to the right of the stone enclosure. Continue down the path to the head of the lake. Go through the gate and down the road following instructions for the walk around Llyn Crafnant on page 104.

Dolwyddelan

Dolwyddelan lies in the lovely Lledr valley at the foot of Moel Siabod. It escaped the tourist boom which affected other villages in the 19th century and is unassuming and un-commercialized. It has a long history. The Roman road Sarn Helen followed this part of the valley and St Gwyddelan founded his church here in the 6th century. Dolwyddelan Castle, 1 kilometre to the west, was built in the 12th century. The village expanded in the 19th century as a slate quarrying village, but today grass and moss are spreading over the grey slate tips. Dolwyddelan makes a good centre for quieter walks in a less frequented area.

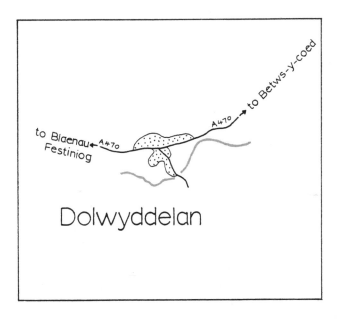

The Lledr Valley Walk

An easy walk along clear tracks to enjoy good views of the Lledr Valley and the mountains.

Distance: 7 kilometres / 4½ miles

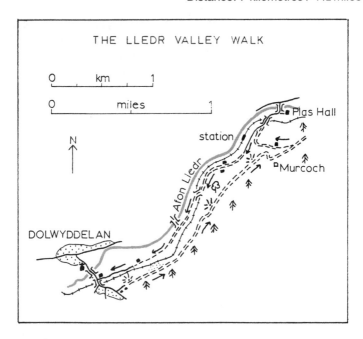

DIRECTIONS: **Dolwyddelan to Bwlch Bach:** Leave the A470 in the centre of Dolwyddelan to turn left (if approaching from Betws-y-coed). Cross two bridges, Pont-y-Llan over the Afon Lledr and the railway bridge (ignoring the left hand turn of your return route). Immediately after the railway bridge turn left, then follow the main road uphill passing the cottages. At the end of the terrace on your right, turn left along the track. Cross a stile (to the left of a gate) to follow a forestry track straight ahead through old slate tips.

Standing on the site of the old Ty'n-y-bryn quarry you

already have a good view over Dolwyddelan. The village is dwarfed by Moel Siabod to the north. Look for the square keep of the 12th century castle to the left (with the slopes of Snowdon as a backdrop).

Continue along the gated forestry road for the next 3 kilometres. You pass through patches of forest but in between there are splendid viewpoints in areas of pasture and open woodland of beech and birch.

However far you walk Moel Siabod is always looking over your shoulder like 'big brother'. You get the distinct impression that here is a mountain which moves! The route of the Roman Road Sarn Helen from Betws-y-coed, and the route of the drovers' roads coming from Capel Curig enter the valley to the east of the mountains.

You can safely put the book away and enjoy the views. Refer to it again when the road swings in a very tight bend into the hillside, with a renovated farmhouse in a field to the right of the road on the edge of the forest.

The ruin of Murcoch in 1987

Continuing along the forest track, turn a corner to enter coniferous forest over a stile to the left of a gate. 175 metres further along the road turn left at a sharp angle to follow a stony path down the slope, passing on your right the large house of Bwlch Bach. The path widens to a track as it winds downhill to a road.*

[A detour is possible to Plas Hall Hotel, open to non-residents. Turn right for 100 metres.]

The Return to Dolwyddelan: Turn left to follow the tarmac road between the base of the hill and the railway line. You will pass Pont-y-pant station (this is a halt only: you will need to hail the train if you wish to speed up your journey back!) After a gate the road becomes a dirt track, then becomes grassy at the top of the hill for a short distance. After a second gate, bear right under the railway line, through a third gate, then bear left to follow the grassy track which parallels the river. Do not turn right to cross the bridge (which once carried a slate tramway) but continue along the track keeping the Afon Lledr on your right.

The track passes through the yard of Ty Isaf farm and past the village football field to arrive at the school, sited between two bridges which you crossed on your outward journey. Turn right to the centre of the village, passing on your left the church of St Gwyddelan.

Dolwyddelan Castle Walk

This gentle walk follows the valley of the Afon Lledr and you are rewarded with spectacular views of the mountains with minimum effort. The walk passes the historic Dolwyddelan Castle, for which there is a small charge, then wanders to the remote end of the valley before returning on a very old paved route way.

> Distance: Shorter loop: 5 km / 3 miles
> Longer loop: 9 km / 5½ miles

For map, see page 62

DIRECTIONS: **From Dolwyddelan to Blaenau Dolwyddelan:** From the village take the main road in the Blaenau Ffestiniog direction towards Dolwyddelan Castle. 200 metres after the lay-by, go through the gate and follow the signposted old track. Through a second gate, turn left if you need a ticket to visit the castle before carrying straight on up the road to the castle.

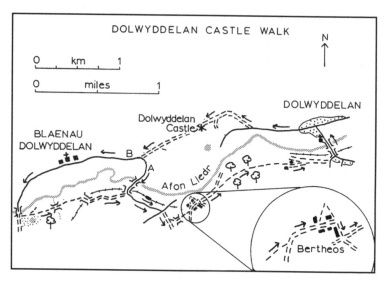

DOLWYDDELAN CASTLE WALK

DOLWYDDELAN CASTLE

Dolwyddelan Castle is a Welsh Castle, built at the end of the 12th century by Iorwerth of the broken nose, and there is a tradition that it is the birth place of his son, Prince Llywelyn the Great. The castle consists of two towers connected by walls enclosing a courtyard. Only one tower remains. It has the ideal site for guarding the old route from Nant Conwy to Meirionnydd.

Where the tarmac stops, take the left, muddier and less obvious track which skirts the base of the hill on which the castle stands. The track passes through a gap in a stone wall and rises up a small pass, below the telegraph wires. At the top of the rise, cross the stile and continue across open moorland. Go through another gate as the track continues with a fence on your right. Pass through three more gates and stiles.

As you walk through these fields you may catch a glimpse of Snowdon ahead to your right while Moel Siabod still dominates the skyline on the right.

At the farm (dogs are tied up!) join the road. If you require the shorter walk, turn left down the road and then follow the directions from the * on page 64.

For the longer walk, turn right along the road and continue for about 1 kilometre to the hamlet of Blaenau Dolwyddelan.

This cluster of houses and chapels has a timeless quality about it. On the edge of the floodplain of the Afon Lledr it has retained its old-world atmosphere as the road leads to a dead-end valley. An example of how the way of life has changed is that the number of ruined or converted chapels almost outnumber the houses!

Continue for a further 700 metres taking the left fork at the road junction. Carry on to the end of the tarmaced road just past the ruins of the quarrymen's houses.

Blaenau Dolwyddelan to Dolwyddelan: Go through the gate and cross the river. Immediately beyond the river, turn left over the stile and take the path along the top of the slate spoil heap parallel with the river.

Here you are walking on an artificial landscape created out of slate waste. You pass a pool on your right, now partly hidden by the birch trees which are already colonising the slate on a minimum of soil.

Follow the signpost which leads through a gate and off the end of the spoil heap and continue straight on with the steep bank on your right and the river on your left. As the field narrows, 30 metres before its end, take the indistinct path uphill through the trees over the rocks to the wall and cross the stile.

Across this field the path is rather indistinct but bears right to cross the ditch by a slate slab and then continues to the bridge with stone walls (ignoring the stile and bridge on your left). From this bridge follow the track to the stone railway bridge. After crossing the railway line go through the gate and turn left along the track which passes to the right of the farm buildings (the dogs are tied up). Continue to the road at the hairpin. Take the right hand fork uphill where you pass, on your left, an oxbow lake – an abandoned loop of the Afon Lledr.

* Carry on to the main road (A470). ! Cross straight over to the road opposite and, about 30 metres along it, take the path leading off to the left by the stream. It follows the stream bank, crossing a tributary before crossing the main stream by an old slate bridge with some sheep enclosures on the opposite bank. Go through the metal gate and continue straight up to the stile. Bear right uphill to the grassy track. Turn left to follow it to Bertheos Farm.

At the farm, go through the left hand gate into the farmyard. Pass between the farm buildings and go straight on to the next gate. Beyond this gate turn right along the grassy path with barns to your right. Go through the gateway, cross the stream and turn left along the track. Follow the track for 200 metres to a gate with a private sign. Fork right along the signposted path, which rises diagonally up the hill. This path soon becomes a track and passes through one gate. At the end of the fence on your right, carry straight on along the path with the wall on your left. Cross a stile to dip down, entering woodland with the wall continuing on your left.

Carry on along the slate path through the trees and fields for about 700 metres. ! The slabs of rock can be very slippery when wet. Cross the wooden bridge and the stile leading into the corner of the next field. About 30 metres beyond the stile a wall joins on the right. Head towards an isolated tree, passing to the right of it. Continue downhill, cross the stile, and pass to the left of the barn.

Go through the two gates ahead, down the track past the house and continue straight on with the railway line on your left. At the road turn left, then left again crossing the railway line. Carry on for about 100 metres to St Gwyddelan Church.

On your left is the little church of St Gwyddelan. Built by Meredydd ap Ieuan in 1512, parts of the building are believed to have been moved from an older church about a quarter of a mile away. He feared the wooded site of the old building might allow bandits to ambush him on his way to worship. Inside is a beautifully carved oak screen from the 15th century and a bronze bell dating from the 6th century. Open every day except Saturday.

The brass of Meredydd ap Ieuan who built St Gwyddelan's church.

The carving of a 'dragon' in St Gwyddelan's Church. It may represent the 'afanc' or water monster which was thought to have caused disastrous floods in the Lledr valley.

From the church gate turn left and you soon return to your starting point, in the centre of the village.

Dolwyddelan to Gwybrnant

This longer walk follows the lovely Lledr Valley before rising to explore the secluded valley of Gwybrnant. You return over the high moor enjoying wide mountain views and a 'top of the world' feeling. This is a favourite walk, full of variety and interest. Gwybrnant (pronounced Goo-ib-er-nant) is famous as the birthplace, at Ty Mawr, of William Morgan. The walk follows the dramatic Lledr gorge for a short distance. Directions are also given for a detour as the gorge section has steep drops. Choose a clear day to appreciate fully the views over the mountains.

Distance: 13 km / 8 miles

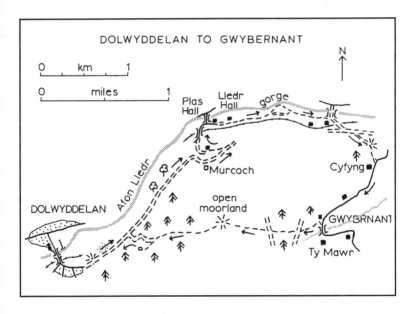

DIRECTIONS: Follow the directions given on pages 58 to 60, as far as the *. Bear right for 130 metres towards Plas Hall. Where the road turns to cross the river, leave it to continue over a slight rise to the right of Plas Hall (walking man sign). When you reach the entrance to Lledr Hall Education Centre continue straight on downhill following a walled track passing Butterpont Cottage. Go straight across at a cross roads where a drive crosses the track, following a public way sign to continue through a gate.

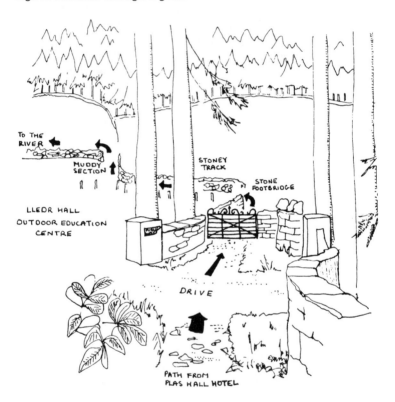

After 10 metres turn left to follow a stony track along a stream bed for 50 metres; the black and white building of Lledr Hall is to the left. The path curves to the right following a field wall (on the right), then swings to the left (wall on the left) towards the river. Here the Afon Lledr foams into a wide pool.

Follow the river downstream along an inviting path between the river and a wall bordering the railway for 600 metres. In some sections the path is walled, in others there is a shallow drop directly to the river.

Where the path rises away from the river and enters a planted area through a second wooden gate, you have a choice to make.

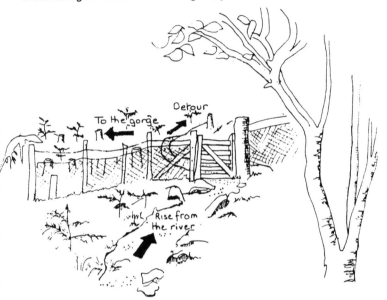

The public footpath bears left to follow for a short way the edge of the Lledr Gorge where flurries of white water cascade into deep turquoise pools beneath sheer rock buttresses. ! It is a rough path and there are steep drops into the river. Detour on page 70.

Enter the felled area through a wooden gate and turn left down the slope. After 10 metres bear right. The path winds through trees, gradually approaching the river bank. Keep left to reach the river and follow the edge of the gorge.

The metal ladders fixed to the side of the gorge in precarious positions were installed for intrepid fishermen to catch salmon and eels. ! They are unsafe.

At a small cliff and stream, the path rises above the gorge and parallels the river. After passing through a wall opening the path rises gently away from the river, to join another path. Turn left to follow it down the slope through a wall opening and over a stepped stile to leave the forest.

The young trees with large oak-shaped leaves are red oaks introduced from America.

[**Detour to avoid the gorge section:** From the wooden gate follow the path through the conifers with walls on both sides. At the end of the wall on your **left**, fork left on a permissive path. As it descends the slope there are views to the left of the cascading river. At the base of the slope, pass through a wall opening and cross a stepped stile to leave the forest.]

From the stepped stile, a stone-flagged path borders the river. Pass farm buildings and a caravan to your right and continue on the path to reach Tan Aeldroch Farm. Go through a gate to continue along the track ahead. Cross the drive and the stepped stile ahead to walk up the clear walled grassy track. Cross a stile by a gate, pass under the railway bridge and bear left up a slope through beech trees to join a forestry track.

Cross the track diagonally to continue along the path which climbs up the slope between deciduous trees on the right and conifers on the left. Where the path touches the edge of the forest there is a good view down the Lledr Valley towards its confluence with the Conwy.

The path widens over a rise, descending to exit via a gate to the left of the building Cyfyng. This was the former chapel and school for the area where the school desks were reversed to use as pews on Sundays. Turn right.

In the Gwybrnant: This steep road climbs into the Gwybrnant, the valley of the viper. To the left are the waterfalls on the Afon Wybr.

The viper in Welsh legend is no ordinary snake for it can sprout wings to become dragon-like. The legend tells that a man intent on killing the viper first consulted a wizard, who told him on three separate occasions that he would die from a viper's bite, break his neck and drown. The man, not believing these conflicting predictions, climbed the rocks in search of the viper. He was bitten by the viper and fell, breaking his neck and falling helplessly into the Afon Wybr to drown.

After a steep climb of 500 metres the road levels out.

You notice a change in the landscape as you enter the gentler slopes of the valley left 'hanging' as the Lledr Valley was deepened further by glaciers during the Ice Ages. The old barns in the Gwybrnant are a reminder of the times when cattle were more important than sheep in the region.

Continue along this gated road to Pwll-y-gath Farm adjacent to the road on your right. Within 50 metres the path back to Dolwyddelan climbs the hill to the right. [Continue along the road if you wish to see the National Trust property of Ty Mawr.]

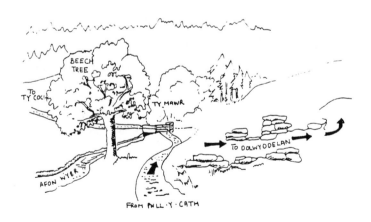

FROM PWLL·Y·CATH

BISHOP MORGAN'S HOUSE
GWYBRNANT

William Morgan was born in Ty Mawr in about 1545. His translation of the Bible into Welsh in 1588 established a standard Welsh from the many local dialects. A National Trust property, Ty Mawr re-opened after restoration in Easter 1988 for the 4th centenary of the Bible's publication. Open April – October, Thursday – Sunday.

The Return to Dolwyddelan: Just before a gate and 50 metres beyond Pwll-y-gath turn right at a sharp angle to follow a broken walled track up the slope. 50 metres up the slope go through a gate then turn left to continue uphill keeping a field wall to your left. The first part of this walk is followed by the nature trail from Ty Mawr and is marked by posts with red discs. It becomes a walled path as it continues up the slope. Pass over a stile onto moorland, a previously felled area.

Where you meet a forestry track, turn right for less than 10 metres, then left at a sharp angle to continue up the path. At the first path junction, take either route as the rejoin. Thereafter, ignore wall openings and keep to the stony path which is bordered by walls and a wealth of mosses.

Cross straight over at the second track and continue up the stony path across moorland, a felled area with scattered young pine trees. The path winds up the slope passing close to two patches of mature conifers on your left. After the second clump of trees, cross the stile onto true moorland.

At first the stone-flagged path is quite clear as it rises over a rocky knoll. The view on a clear day is glorious. Moel Siabod towers ahead and to the left are the Snowdon Horseshoe and Yr Aran. Follow the diagrams to find your way over the moor. The path clings to the left of two large mounds with boggy patches in between where the path is indistinct.

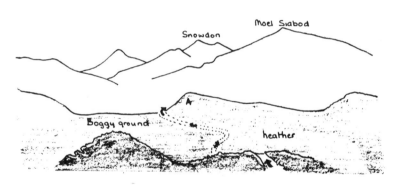

Facing the peaks of Snowdon, walk to the left
of the projecting mound A.

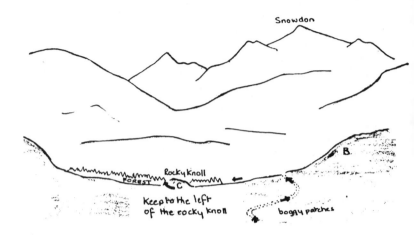

Continue to the left of the next mound B. Ahead and to your left lies a rocky knoll C. Pass to the left of it and continue downhill to enter a coniferous plantation.

Walk down the hill through a forest plantation for one kilometre. Only one path leaves the main track to lead off to the left near the lower edge of the forest. Do not follow it but keep to the more steeply sloping unsigned path for a further 100 metres to a gateway at the forest boundary. From here you look down towards Dolwyddelan.

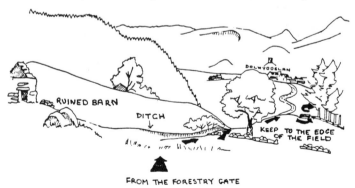

74

Walk straight ahead across the corner of a field to a 'ditch' (a stream running in what may have been a sunken track). Keep this 'ditch' to your left as you walk along the edge of the adjoining field to a gateway by a grove of conifers. Continue straight down the path with the fence to your left. Where it joins a grassy track, turn left. This track zigzags down the slope, skirting the boundary of the forest. Where it ends at a broken gate, bear right to follow a rocky track (adopted by the stream) for 100 metres to meet the forestry track of your outward journey.

Turn left to return to Dolwyddelan for 750 metres on the forest road. At a road junction turn right downhill. Turn right again to cross two bridges and continue to the village centre, passing on your left the village church of St Gwyddelan which is well-worth a visit (information on pages 65 and 66). There are tea rooms and an inn, 'Y Gwydyr', at the crossroads.

Llanberis

Llanberis, on the shores of Llyn Padarn and at the entrance to the dramatic Llanberis Pass, is dominated by the slate quarries which gave rise to its growth. The Snowdon mountain railway starts here and there is a second narrow gauge railway running alongside the lake. There is a Welsh slate museum and a branch of the National Museum of Wales, Oriel Eryri. On the outskirts of the town stands the tower of Dolbadarn, a Welsh 12th century castle. There is little evidence of one of the largest engineering schemes in Europe, the Dinorwic Hydro-electric Pumped Storage System buried in huge caverns under Elidir Fach. A park borders the lake and there are plenty of tearooms and inns. A car park is sited on the shores of Llyn Padarn (on the by-pass).

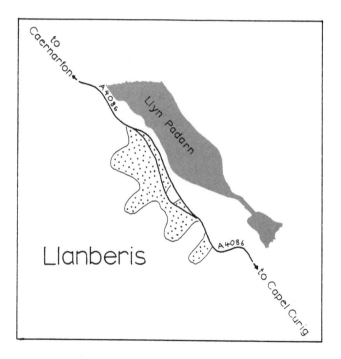

The Llanberis Loop

This short walk rises up onto moorland above the village following clear tracks past farms which flourished in time gone by. On a clear day views of the majestic mountain of Snowdon can be obtained above the expanse of moorland, in contrast with the village nestling in the valley below.

Distance: 5 km / 3 miles

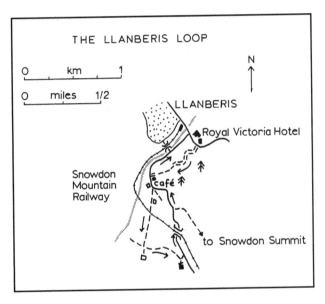

DIRECTIONS: Follow the main road from Llanberis in the Capel Curig direction. Just past the Royal Victoria Hotel, turn right at the forest track, climb the stile and follow the track through the conifers. The route winds uphill passing a kissing gate towards the top of the forest where it follows, for 75 metres, an old tramway which pre-dates the plantation. Pass through two more kissing gates and follow the path in front of the house to the road. Turn left uphill for 150 metres, passing a ruin on your right, and, at the left hand bend in the road by a strange slate structure, turn right through a gap in the wall. Head towards the next ruin, keeping the wall on your left. Continue along this path beyond the ruin and cross the railway. ! Look out for trains.

This rack and pinion railway is the Snowdon Mountain Railway, constructed in 1901, providing the easy way to the summit of Wales' highest mountain. On its inaugural trip the carriages, which in those days were pulled by the engine, broke away and started to roll down the hill out of control. One man panicked and jumped out, falling to his death on the rocks below. The carriages eventually came to rest with all the remaining passengers safely inside.

Climb the stile and carry on across the moor on a clear path towards Cae Newydd, the ruined farmhouse among the trees, 450 metres ahead.

Looking around you, there are numerous scattered buildings but few are now lived in indicating the decline of population in the rural uplands. Despite many drainage ditches dug with the help of EU subsidies, the grazing here remains poor.

As you near the bridge over the stream, the path veers to the right towards it. On joining the main track turn left along it (away from the stream). Ahead of you is Snowdon with Elidir Fach over to the left above the quarry. Cross the stile over the fence and follow the track uphill to the old building.

This used to be a chapel for the scattered community. ! Do not enter the building as the floor is rotten, but if you look in the doorway there are still the remains of the old plaster and paintwork, its presence reinforces the feeling of history in the area.

Cross the stile to your left and turn left down the road. Follow the road downhill for 1.5 kilometres crossing underneath the Snowdon Railway and passing the end of the Llanberis Path which leads to Snowdon Summit. Continue to the main road and turn left to return to the village.

The Waterfalls and Hill Fort Walk

Beginning in the village centre, this short walk rises to over 1000 feet to an iron-age hill fort affording panoramic views of Western Snowdonia. It passes en route the beautiful Ceunant Mawr Waterfalls and the Snowdon Mountain Railway.

Distance: 5 km / 3 miles

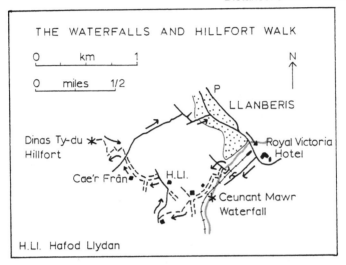

DIRECTIONS: Take the main road in the Capel Curig direction and turn right along Victoria Terrace, opposite the Royal Victoria Hotel. Take the first turning on the right, signposted to the waterfalls, and 50 metres beyond the viaduct bear left. 30 metres beyond this, a signposted road goes off to the left over a cattle grid. Follow the road up for 300 metres, past the cottages, to the viewpoint of the waterfall which is reached by crossing the narrow gauge Snowdon Railway.! Look out for trains.

These falls, called Ceunant Mawr, occur where the Afon Arddu has cut a small ravine. The upper valley was formed by a small tributary glacier feeding a major glacier in the Llanberis Pass. After the ice melted, the tributary valley was left 'hanging' above the main one, thus forming a cliff for the waterfall.

79

Continue up the road and, after about 50 metres, take the right hand fork. After 100 metres, turn through the kissing gate on your left and walk up the hill keeping the wall on your right. Go through a gap in the wall ahead. Continue uphill, ignoring the grassy track leading off left, and follow round the right hand edge of the field. Cross the small stream and turn right through the kissing gate. Follow the stream across the field and go through a second kissing gate in the corner. Follow the edge of this field keeping the wall on your left until you reach the road.

Turn right down the road for about 800 metres. At the end of the wall on your right, made out of large rocks, an old track goes off to the left opposite farm buildings. Turn left along this track for 30 metres to a stile on your left. Cross the stile and then follow the clear track across two fields passing in front of the farmhouse of Cae'r Frân. Continue on a slate path up to the narrow tarmac road and cross it.

Go through the sheep pens opposite and bear right through the bracken on a narrow path which joins a more distinct path leading uphill. The path zigzags up the steep slope crossing straight over another path till you reach a wall with a gate in it. Remaining on this side of the wall, turn right and continue upwards following the wall for 100 metres. Then turn left up to the summit.

Here are the remains of Dinas Ty Du (Black House City) an iron-age hill fort. Its superb defensive position is obvious, but scattered stones are all that remain of the original stone wall encircling the fort. To the north lie Llyn Padarn and the village of Llanberis 700 feet below, with Llyn Peris at the foot of the slate quarries. To the east lies Snowdon with its dramatic glaciated hollows. To the west, over the scattered spoil heaps from the slate quarries, there are views of Anglesey and the Irish Sea.

Return from the summit by the same way to the road. Turn left down the road for 800 metres to the end and at the T-junction turn right. At the next T-junction turn left and follow this road to return to the village.

Dolbadarn Castle and Quarry Walk

This walk explores a way of life which has long since disappeared from the area. It climbs through the slate quarries which dominate Llanberis, passing the slate museum and quarry hospital, and finally reaches the village above the quarry. The walk incorporates the most interesting aspects of the industry, but also visits the 12th century Welsh Dolbadarn Castle and passes through native oak woodland. Although not a long walk, it rises up 600 feet on clear paths to give views of Llyn Padarn and Llanberis.

Distance: 7.5 km / 4 miles

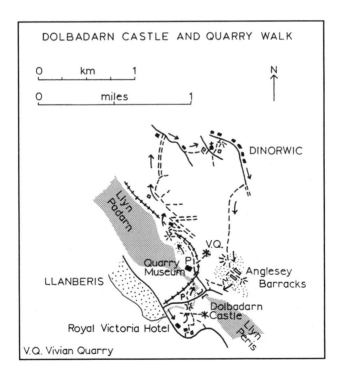

DOLBADARN CASTLE AND QUARRY WALK

0   km   1

0   miles   1

N

DINORWIC

Llyn Padarn

V.Q.

Quarry Museum

LLANBERIS

Anglesey Barracks

Dolbadarn Castle

Royal Victoria Hotel

Llyn Peris

V.Q. Vivian Quarry

DIRECTIONS: **Llanberis to the Slate Quarry:** Take the main road from the village towards Capel Curig for 450 metres, and just past the Royal Victoria Hotel turn left through the gate with a large slate post. Wind round the edge of the hotel car park, bear right and, keeping the old wall to your left, go through the metal kissing gate. Skirt round the right hand edge of the wood and cross the main path. A gate marks the path leading up to the castle.

This Welsh Castle was built probably in the late 12th century by Llywelyn ap Iorwerth (Iorwerth of the broken nose) who also constructed Dolwyddelan Castle (page 63). It guards the entrance to the Llanberis Pass and over the years has been used as a prison. Owain Glyndwr, leader of uprisings in the 1400's, imprisoned Lord Grey of Ruthin here before himself being defeated and imprisoned.

Return to the gate on the perimeter fence of the castle and pass through the gap in the wall opposite, to the left of the 'bus shelter'. Enter the wood and take the path to the right down some steps. Cross the river and enter the car park opposite. Go through right hand kissing gate adjacent to the signboard and follow the path under the railway bridge ahead. Turn right over the river and left into the museum car park.

The entrance to Vivian Quarry

Apart from visiting the museum itself on your left, it is worth making a detour into the Vivian Quarry on your right under the bridge across the level crossing. Here the quarry workings have left a spectacular deep blue pool used by divers with dramatic cliff faces often used by climbers.

Slate Quarry to Dinorwic: Continue through the car park keeping the Lakeside Railway on your right. Passing the water sports building on your left, cross over the slate spoil heap following the wide path ahead. Climb up the steps on to the old hospital terrace from which the whole of Llyn Padarn and Llanberis village can be seen.

The hospital itself is worth visiting, as it illustrates many of the hazards of working in the slate quarries. Some of the equipment there looks more like instruments of torture rather than implements used for first aid purposes!

From the hospital leave by the main gates (to your right) and immediately turn left, doubling back up the hill behind the building (signposted with footprints). Follow the track round the first hairpin bend and, about 80 metres beyond the bend, a path doubles back to the left up the hill. Take this, rising above the hospital and the lake; both should be just visible through the oak trees. Climb on up for about 200 metres to the viewpoint. Here the path bears right and continues upwards. 20 metres beyond the viewpoint carry straight on ignoring another path which joins it from the right. 100 metres further on take the right fork, continuing uphill, through the gap in the wall to a junction in paths at a tree stump. Bear left here walking slightly downhill. The main path wanders on for 350 metres to a solid metal gate where you leave the Padarn Country Park. Keeping the unusual slate fence on your right you soon cross a bridge over a stream. Go through the metal gate and continue straight up the walled track to the road. Turn right along the road for 300 metres and, just beyond the cottage on your left, turn left through the gate. Cross the field keeping the fence on your right, bear right in front of the old cottage, then turn left just beyond it. Keeping the wall on your left the path brings you onto the road opposite a large slate-hung chapel. Turn right past the chapel and then immediately left by the footpath sign.

As you pass the ruined cottages you see a whole landscape which is the remnant of a past era. There is no clustered village, only scattered small-holdings comprising Dinorwic where the quarrymen attempted to supplement their meagre income. The innumerable footpaths indicate how each miner found the quickest route to his home.

Dinorwic to Llanberis: At the top you can just catch a glimpse of the sea over to your left before turning right along the road. Walking along this road, you pass the reclaimed spoil heaps where the landscape has been 'improved'. Keep round to the right on this new road to where it returns to the old road at a 'No Through Road' sign.

The road deteriorates to a track continuing past a row of cottages, ignoring private drives. After 400 metres the track ends; continue straight ahead down the footpath and the steps through the trees. It is worth making a detour to the left to 'Anglesey Barracks', the double row of ruined cottages.

Anglesey Barracks were named after the men who lived here. Unemployment was such a problem on the island that some men would even walk from Anglesey to Llanberis on Monday mornings, living in the barracks all week, working long hours on the quarry faces. They returned home on Saturday afternoons to stay with their families on Sunday, most of which most probably would have been spent in chapel.

Return to the path and continue down the slope crossing the metal bridge over the old tramway. Continue walking down the slate spoil heap by means of the walled path.

Llyn Peris can be seen clearly with its artificial slate banks designed to cope with the daily fluctuating levels of water. It is the lower reservoir in the Dinorwic Pumped Storage Power Station which produces electricity by day and pumps water back at night to the upper reservoir of Marchlyn Mawr. The whole of the power station is in an enormous underground hole to your left. Three million tonnes of slate have been removed to create the cavern which is twice the length and half the width of a soccer pitch and is higher than a 16-storey building.

Continue down this zigzagging path to a gap in the wall on your left. Turn left and carry on down through the trees, in places on steep steps. At the road, turn right to the junction, then left to the main road on the outskirts of Llanberis.

Llanrwst

Llanrwst is the market town for the Conwy Valley, the hub of a busy farming region. It has a lovely setting on the eastern bank of the Afon Conwy. It is a historic town; Llanrwst Bridge (Pont Fawr), designed by Inigo Jones, was for two centuries the main crossing point of the river. Many of the old industries including harp-making have died but there is plenty to explore. Missed by many tourists to the area, it is well worth a visit. Early closing is on Thursday. There is a large car park to the right of the A470 on entering Llanrwst from the north, and another over Pont Fawr by the recreation ground. A third car park lies to the left of Watling Street. Parking in the Market Square is limited. Three short walks are described here. For longer walks cross the valley floor via Gowers bridge (see page 88) to Trefriw. (Walks from Trefriw page 96). Llanrwst is not a village but a town!!

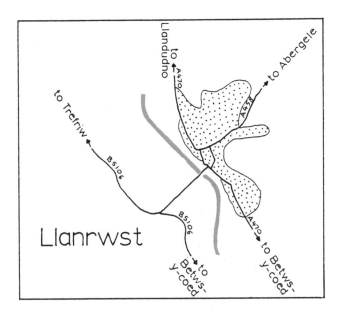

A Walk on the Pastures of Nant Conwy

A short peaceful walk over the valley fields away from traffic. Avoid the area when the river is high for this part of the valley is subject to spectacular flooding (mostly in winter). It is very easy to follow: keep turning right.

For map, see page 88   Distance: 3 km / 1¾ miles

DIRECTIONS: From Ancaster Square walk towards the river, downhill from the pedestrian crossing.

Cross Llanrwst Bridge to Ty Hwnt i'r Bont.

Designed by Inigo Jones, this beautiful bridge was built in 1636. It was for many years the main bridge over the Conwy (the 'Pont Fawr', the large, important bridge). A sundial on the parapet was added to mark three centuries of use.

Ty Hwnt i'r Bont is the old courthouse and is an excellent stop for coffee and fresh scones (closed during the winter months).

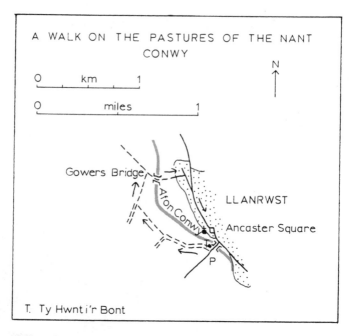

A WALK ON THE PASTURES OF THE NANT CONWY

Gowers Bridge
Afon Conwy
LLANRWST
Ancaster Square
P
T. Ty Hwnt i'r Bont

Behind Ty Hwnt i'r Bont a track leads away from the right hand side of the road (walking man sign). Follow this sometimes muddy track over the flat valley fields. To the right is a good view of St Crwst's Church on the opposite side of the river.

> *St Crwst was the celtic saint who gave Llanrwst its name (Llan, an enclosure near a church). It has a fine Renaissance chapel in which lies Prince Llywelyn's stone coffin and some brasses of the Wyn family.*

After 500 metres, where the track curves sharply to the left, cross the stepped stile to the right of the gate into the valley fields. The footpath follows the right hand boundary of the next three adjoining fields. In the right hand corners of each there is a wooden stile. The fourth field is a smaller one. Again keep to the right hand boundary but this time leave the field in the right hand corner over a concrete bridge and wooden stile to join an overgrown grassy track. Bear right to cross a stile on the right hand fence on top of the embankment.

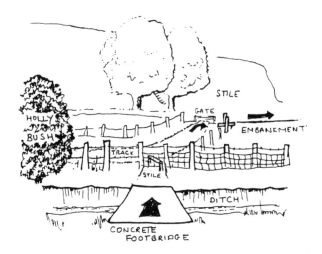

The valley sides differ in geology and land use. This section of the Conwy Valley follows a fault line between older, more resistant rocks of the Ordovician age (over 400 million years old) to your left, and younger less resistant Silurian rocks to your right.

Follow the path which runs along the top of this perfectly straight embankment to Gower's Bridge.

This embankment is part of the flood control scheme frequently needed in this area.
John Gower was a rector of Trefriw who provided for the original bridge and road to be built to help people to reach Trefriw (growing as a Victorian spa) from Llanrwst railway station.

Turn right over the bridge and turn immediately right again over a wooden stile. Turn left along the river bank. Keep the river on your right all the way back to Llanrwst Bridge, joining a board walk for part of the way.

A Walk above Llanrwst

A short walk following good tracks and paths to enjoy views over Llanrwst, the Conwy Valley and the hills to the west.

Distance: 3.5 km / 2¼ miles

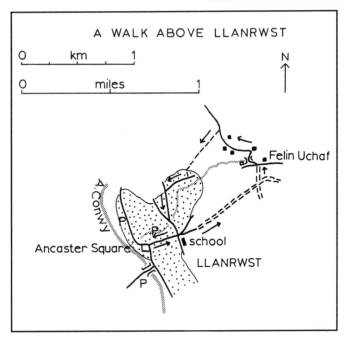

DIRECTIONS: From Ancaster Square turn right into Denbigh Street continuing to the crossroads at the base of the hill. Turn right and immediately left to walk up Town Hill. At first a tarmaced road flanked by houses, it soon changes to a quiet, un-surfaced, sometimes muddy track as it climbs the hill. This is the old road out of Llanrwst.

As the track reaches the brow of the hill it levels out and starts a slow descent. The pastures of the hill farms rise in green waves before you. Near the base of the dip, at cross roads, turn left to follow a dirt track for 200 metres to an A-road. ! Cross this busy road with care to a single storey white cottage, Felin Uchaf.

Turn sharply to the left in front of the cottage to follow a road into a deep narrow valley with the ruins of a solidly built corn mill by the bridge.

The road climbs out of the valley shadows, passing several houses, and levels out.

> *You can now enjoy views over Llanrwst and the hills to the west rising to the Carneddau. Behind you, to the left you look towards the upper Conwy Valley and Betws-y-coed.*

Look for a gate on the left of the road opposite the entrance to a house, Tyn Gwern Ucha, standing above the road on the right. 100 metres further on is a second gate. Beside it (to the left) is a kissing gate, the start of the return journey downhill.

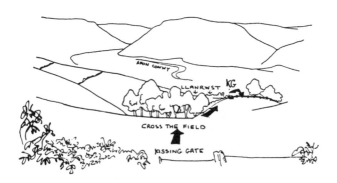

Walk diagonally across the field, towards a line of trees and go through the kissing gate. Follow the left hand boundary to a second kissing gate in the far corner of the field. Continue down the left hand boundary of the next steep field to another kissing gate. This leads to a path between a fence and a hedge to a fourth kissing gate into a recreation area.

Keep to the left of the recreation area. Turn left along a path flanked by houses and then right continuing through the housing estate on the main route. Bear left down a slope to meet a minor road. Go straight ahead to reach the crossroads which you will recognise as the start of your walk up the hill. Turn right to return to Ancaster Square.

Afon Conwy and Gwydir Castle Walk

A short interesting walk which follows the river as it crosses the valley pastures to the western slope. You can get a glimpse back in time by visiting Gwydir Uchaf Chapel with its fine mediaeval painted ceiling and Gwydir Castle, home in the past of the Wynn family, the local landed gentry. (There are charges for admission to both. They are open Tuesday – Friday and Sunday, 10am – 4pm; key for the chapel available from the castle. Tel: 01492 641687). The walk follows well-made paths and tracks and the only uphill section is a gentle climb. ! There is no pavement bordering the B-road which you follow for 400 metres. This walk is impassable at times of flood.

For map, see page 93   Distance: 4 km / 2½ miles

DIRECTIONS: Cross Llanrwst Bridge and immediately turn left to follow a riverside path bordering the recreation ground.

> *The stone circle in the park is not an ancient one. It commemorates the holding of the National Eisteddfod here in 1951 and again in 1989.*

The path leads through a kissing gate to continue between the river and a bordering wall. Pass a metal stile, now obsolete.

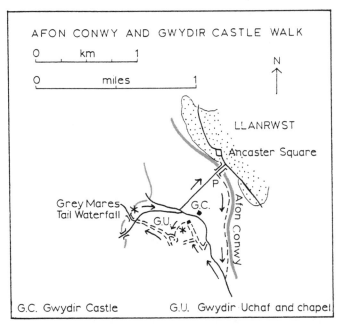

AFON CONWY AND GWYDIR CASTLE WALK

LLANRWST

Ancaster Square

Grey Mares Tail Waterfall

G.C.

G.U.

Afon Conwy

G.C. Gwydir Castle   G.U. Gwydir Uchaf and chapel

There are the remains of a quay on the riverside where the river starts to ripple after a still section. The barges, which supplied Llanrwst before the coming of the railway, turned here before returning downstream.

The path follows the river, running along the top of the river embankment.

There are three wooden stiles to cross along the embankment. Having crossed the third, bear right over a small stream to cross diagonally up the field to a small metal gate leading onto the road. Turn right to follow this B-road for 400 metres. ! This is a narrow section with no pavement.

Passing a spring and a drinking trough on your left, turn left to follow the sign to 'Gwydir Uchaf Chapel'. A curving tarmac road leads up the slope to Gwydir Uchaf, now the offices of the Forest Enterprise. Turn left to follow the gravel path running alongside the chapel.

Gwydir Uchaf was much larger when it was built by Sir John Wynn in 1604 with extensive formal gardens stretching round the hillside. The private chapel was built in 1673 by Sir Richard Wynn. It has a remarkable ceiling painted by an unknown local artist. There is a stepped ornamental mound behind the chapel from which the Wynn family enjoyed views of the valley.

Continue up the walled track, past a wooden hut on your right, and go through two kissing gates to join a forestry track. Turn right and right again enjoying views of the valley for 500 metres to a crossroads.

The cliffs above are Carreg-y-Gwalch, the refuge of Dafydd ap Siencyn, a Welsh Robin Hood in the 15th century.

Cross straight over at the cross roads taking the road signed to Llanrhychwyn which crosses a stream. Follow the road for 125 metres to a stile. Turn down the footpath to obtain fine views of the Grey Mares Tail Waterfall. Zigzag down the well maintained path and follow it with the stream on your right down to the road.

Turn right along the road. There is no pavement but there is a fairly wide grass verge. At the road junction it is possible to visit Gwydir Castle, with its straying peacocks (opening as for Gwydir Uchaf Chapel). If you wish to detour to visit the 'castle', turn right for 350 metres to the entrance.

Gwydir Castle would more aptly be called a mansion or manor-house. Building began here in the early 16th century and in its day it was considered a great house. The Wynn family had a great influence on the development of the valley; their symbol, the eagle, can be seen in many places around Llanrwst. It is claimed that Queen Elizabeth I and Charles I stayed here. The Cedar of Lebanon in the fine garden was planted to celebrate Charles I wedding. The 'castle' was gutted by fire in the 1920's but is currently being restored to its original state. The panelling for the dining room has recently been reinstated after spending years in storage in New York.

Turn left along the road back to Llanrwst Bridge.

Trefriw

Sited on a rocky step where the Crafnant Valley joins the Conwy, Trefriw is a good walking centre with 'vertical take-off' into the hills. It does not look like a port but river transport was an important reason for its growth in the 19th century and an exporting centre for lead and zinc ores mined in the hills to the west (the old quays can still be seen). Victorian visitors also arrived by boat to 'take the waters', rich in iron and sulphur at the nearby Trefriw Spa. The falls on the Crafnant supply power for the family run woollen mill (est. 1859). There is a car park and W.C.'s opposite the woollen mill shop in the centre of the village.

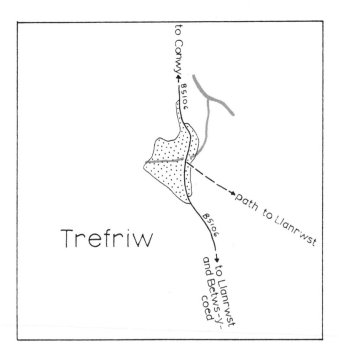

A Walk to Llyn Crafnant and Llyn Geirionydd

This is a long walk to explore the lovely landscape lying to the west of Trefriw. It will occupy an enjoyable day. Hidden in the hills lie two of the loveliest Snowdonia lakes. There is a real sense of discovery when you approach them from any direction. They differ in character. Llyn Crafnant lies deeper in the hills; boats may be hired here for trout fishing, but there is no swimming for the lake is a reservoir. Llyn Geirionydd has a more remote air. There is no fishing here because of the high lead content of the water but windsurfing, speedboats and sailing are allowed. ! Both lakes lie in rock basins deepened by ice action and the ground shelves steeply offshore. There is a seasonal lakeside cafe by Llyn Crafnant, and at Llyn Geirionydd a picnic site and W.C.'s.

For map, see page 98   Distance: 14 km / 9 miles

Because there are car parks by both lakes, shorter walks are possible:

1) a walk around Llyn Crafnant is described on page 104
                                        Distance: 5 km / 3 miles
2) a walk around Llyn Geirionydd is described on page 105
                                        Distance: 3 km / 2 miles
3) a walk around both lakes is described on page 107
                                        Distance: 8 km / 5 miles

DIRECTIONS: **Trefriw to Llyn Geirionydd**: From the car park opposite the woollen mill in the centre of the village turn left onto the main road. Turn to the right up a steep road which borders the village school. As you climb the slope the road bears left passing Bryn Ysgol. Ignore a road joining from the left and continue to a T-junction. Turn left to follow the road up the slope for 100 metres. Before you reach a detached house (Y Wern) on the right of the road, turn right to follow a walking man sign up a path into a coniferous plantation. This well-defined path soon passes, via a wooden stile, into more open

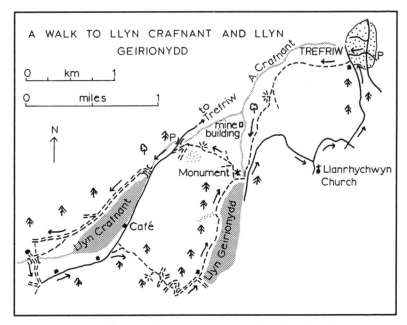

A WALK TO LLYN CRAFNANT AND LLYN GEIRIONYDD

TREFRIW

to Trefriw

A Crafnant

mine building

Monument

Llanrhychwyn Church

Café

Llyn Crafnant

Llyn Geirionydd

N

km

miles

deciduous woodland and rough pasture and begins the slow ascent up the side of the Crafnant Valley. After a steady climb for over 1 kilometre you cross a short boulder strewn section to rise to a good viewpoint. From here you can see the two rock basins in which the lakes lie, separated by the hill of Mynydd Deulyn.

It is hard to imagine that 100 years ago these hills echoed with the noise of industry. Thousands of tonnes of lead and zinc ore were mined in this corner between the Afon Conwy and Afon Llugwy to be exported via Trefriw. In the valley below lie the ruins of an ore processing plant. Ahead on the slopes of Mynydd Deulyn are the black holes of the old Clogwyn y Fuwch slate quarry.

The path continues now turning into the Geirionydd valley. Ignoring a steep path up to your left, your route is now bordered on the left by a field wall with deciduous woodland on the down slope side. It passes through a wooden gate and crosses a wooded gully over a stone footbridge. Emerging from the gully the path levels out for it once carried a tramway for the transport of ores from the New Pandora Mine to the processing plant, the ruins of which lie in the valley below.

> *Look for the leat to the left of the level track which brought water from Llyn Geirionydd for processing and power to the tank immediately above the processing plant.*

Cross two stiles as you follow the path to join the road bordering Llyn Geirionydd. At the lake, turn right through a kissing gate to cross the outlet of the lake. Passing a barn on your left, turn right to walk up a mound to the Taliesin Monument.

Taliesin was a famous bard who wrote by the shores of Llyn Geirionydd in the 6th century.

Llyn Geirionydd to Llyn Crafnant: Descend from Taliesin's Monument; take the grassy track to the left of the monument which leads **away** from the lake. At the top of the grassy slope keep the conifers on your left and descend the stony path. Cross a wooden ladder stile and fork right to follow the path round the slope.

After 30 metres, fork left uphill as the path crosses bracken, then winds through patches of silver birch and hawthorn. Continue over undulating ground, ignoring the path which joins on your left. A rise to a rocky knoll gives a good viewpoint looking down over the smallholdings of the upper Crafnant. To the left are the gaping holes of the old quarries of Clogwyn y Fuwch under Mynydd Deulyn. Continue along the path to pass the ruins of the old works buildings under the quarried crags. Exit via the stile onto a forestry track. Take the right fork downhill, crossing another stile beside a forestry gate to a T-junction.*

Turn left to walk uphill along the road for 500 metres to the shores of Llyn Crafnant.

On the shores of Llyn Crafnant: Turn right to cross the stream flowing from the lake and turn left onto the forestry track which borders the lake shore.

750 metres along the shore, where the forestry track splits on entering coniferous forest, take the lower track to continue along the lake shore.

[In very dry conditions it is possible to take the footpath to the left 600 metres past the track junction. This leads through fields to a stream. Follow the stream up over the bridge. Turn left and follow the instructions from the top of page 101. This is **very** muddy for most of the year.]

Continue up the track which narrows and becomes steeper and rougher. Turn left, just before a bridge, down a steep signed path above Hendre Farm. Cross the stepped stile and continue down to the stream. Turn right, cross the wooden bridge and turn left along the track through the gate.

Hendre and Hafod are common names for farms. Hendre (winter dwelling) and Hafod (summer dwelling) are reminders of the time when farmers moved with their animals to utilize the higher pastures in summer. In the past there were more cattle (needing supervision and milking) than sheep in the hills.

The dirt track crosses the head of the lake for 400 metres. Passing a white modern bungalow in trees to the right, you descend a slight slope.

Hut circle at the head of Llyn Crafnant
(opposite to the white bungalow of Bryn Eithen)

Look in the field to the left to see large stones lying in a horseshoe shape (there is a tree growing in the wall). This is the base of a prehistoric home. These pastures lying in the lap of the craggy hills have been a favoured site for settlements for centuries.

At a T-junction turn left through a metal gate to follow the tarmac road which runs alongside the south eastern side of the valley. Follow the road for 1 kilometre, passing on your left the white building of Maes Mawr and Cornel, now a scout centre, to a telephone kiosk by a former Congregationalist chapel.

From Llyn Crafnant to Llyn Geirionydd: On the opposite side of the road to the telephone kiosk is a ladder stile. Turn right to cross it into a plantation of larch. Turn right at a junction in paths to climb up the slope through heather and plantations of larch and Norway spruce. Look backwards to admire the views over the growing trees towards the crags at the head of Llyn Crafnant.

At the crest of the hill, cross a stile over an old fence and pass through a gap in the wall. [To make a detour to a viewpoint, turn immediately right to a small rocky knoll. There is a good view and a change in the skyline, looking south-eastwards to the smooth outline of the Denbigh Moors.]

From the main path, descend to a forest track and bear right down it for 50 metres. After the junction, turn immediately left down a stony path. Cross straight over the track (1st loop) and descend the muddy path to the 2nd loop of the track. Turn right, then left down the path to the 3rd loop of the track. Here turn left to continue to the base of the slope at the head of Llyn Geirionydd.

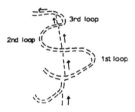

The Western Shore of Llyn Geirionydd: Just as the track turns right to cross the end of the lake, leave it to turn left over a stile to the right of a gate. Walk below the cottage of Ty Newydd to follow the western shore of Llyn Geirionydd. Take the path which crosses the fields bordering the lake. Cross a stile into a larch plantation to continue by the water's edge.

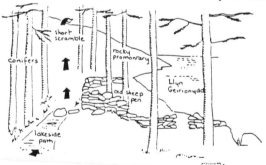

Where you meet a stone wall (an old sheep pen) bear left to clamber over a rocky promontory. On the other side you will find a small cove with a mine adit. ! It is unsafe to enter any of the mine levels.

In the middle of the last century there was a 'lead and zinc rush' in these hills. Here, the mineralized vein runs almost vertically up the hill.

Continue along the lakeshore following the sometimes boggy path. As you near the end of the lake you cross a stile and pass through an open gateway. Just before the second gateway bear right with a wall on your left, passing a barn on the right.

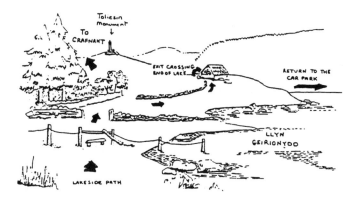

Turn right to cross the outlet of the lake. Through the kissing gate join a tarmac road.

The Return to Trefriw: Turn left to follow this gated road up the hill away from the lake for over 1 kilometre to a T-junction. (If you wish to see Llanrhychwyn Church, make a detour to the right, see page 111). Turn left to walk through Llanrhychwyn. ! Be aware of traffic on this narrow section of road. At a crossroads turn left for 1.5 kilometres to return to Trefriw.

From the plateau of Llanrhychwyn there are views over the Nant Conwy and the eastern slope of the valley and you can understand why traditional life could continue in Llanrhychwyn, protected by its mountain wall from the incursions which affected the valley below.

Turn right at the base of the slope to retrace your steps to the centre of the village.

A Walk around Llyn Crafnant

This is a very easy walk along good tracks. A walk around this peaceful, sheltered lake is a delight at any time of year. There is a lakeside cafe, open in summer, where boats may be hired for fishing but no swimming is allowed.

Distance: 5 km / 3 miles

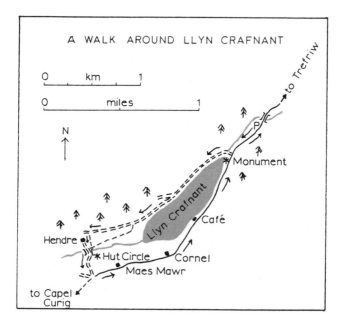

TO THE CAR PARK: Turn up the very steep hill, opposite the Fairy Falls in the centre of Trefriw. The road levels out to climb more gently for about 3 kilometres, where it enters conifers. Turn right into the signed Forest Enterprise car park.

LOOKING TOWARDS THE HEAD OF LLYN CRAFNANT FROM THE LAKESIDE ROAD

DIRECTIONS: From the car park turn right to walk up the road for a further 500 metres to the lake. From here follow the directions under the side heading **On the shores of Llyn Crafnant** on pages 100-101. After passing Maes Mawr and Cornel continue along the lakeside road. 300 metres beyond the telephone kiosk is the lakeside cafe. The road continues to the end of the lake and back to the car park.

A Walk around Llyn Geirionydd

This is a short walk around a beautiful lake. The path on the western side of the lake has a more uneven surface than that around Crafnant and involves one short clamber over a rocky promontory.

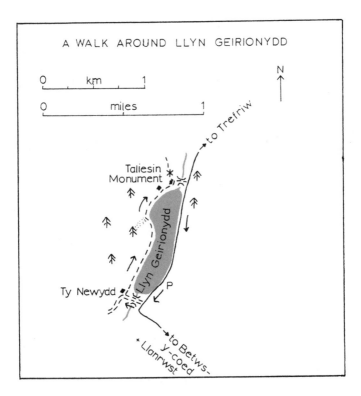

A WALK AROUND LLYN GEIRIONYDD

to Trefriw

Taliesin Monument

Llyn Geirionydd

P

Ty Newydd

to Betws-y-coed

Llanrwst

Distance: 3 km / 2 miles

TO THE CAR PARK: The car park can be approached from Trefriw via Llanrhychwyn, but also from Llanrwst via the Nant Bwlch-yr-Haearn, and from Betws-y-coed via the steep road to the right of the Ugly House.

DIRECTIONS: From the car park on the shore of the lake, turn left along the lakeshore road for 200 metres to the end of the lake. Turn right over a stile beside a forestry gate to cross the causeway at the head of the lake. Do not follow the road up the slope but turn right over a stile to follow a path in front of the cottage of Ty Newydd.

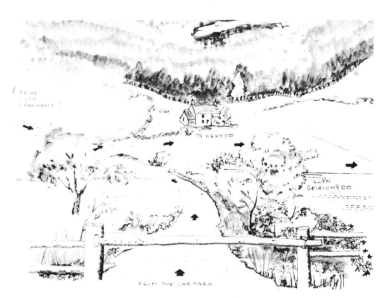

From here follow the directions given on page 102 under the side-heading **The Western Shore of Llyn Geirionydd**. When you rejoin the tarmac road on the other side of the lake, turn right to follow the gated road for 1 kilometre back to the car park.

Llyn Crafnant and Llyn Geirionydd

This is a well-known walk, full of changing terrain and views around both lakes. To save space reference is made to directions given on previous pages.

For map, see page 98   Distance: 8 km / 5 miles

TO THE CAR PARK; Turn up the very steep hill which turns off the main road opposite the Fairy Falls in the centre of Trefriw. The road levels out to climb more gently for about 3 kilometres, where it enters conifers. Turn right into the signed Forest Enterprise car park.

DIRECTIONS: From the car park turn right to walk up the road for a further 500 metres to the lake. Now follow the consecutive directions given under the side-headings. **On the Shores of Llyn Crafnant, From Llyn Crafnant to Llyn Geirionydd, The Western Shore of Llyn Geirionydd** (pages 100-102).

At the end of the lake do not turn right but continue ahead to the Taliesin Monument to return to the Crafnant Valley following the directions on page 100 under the side-heading **Llyn Geirionydd to Llyn Crafnant**, to the asterisk. (Diagram page 103.)

You will find that when you return to the T-junction you are almost opposite the car park.

The Llanrhychwyn Walk

This is a walk up the forested side of the Conwy Valley to the plateau around Llanrhychwyn with its mediaeval church. It is like climbing a beanstalk to another world! The walk continues over Pen-y-Drum with views of the Snowdonia peaks before descending to the shores of Llyn Geirionydd and returning via the Crafnant Valley. You follow quiet paths and tracks to enjoy a variety of landscapes and views. This is a fairly long but generally easy walk.

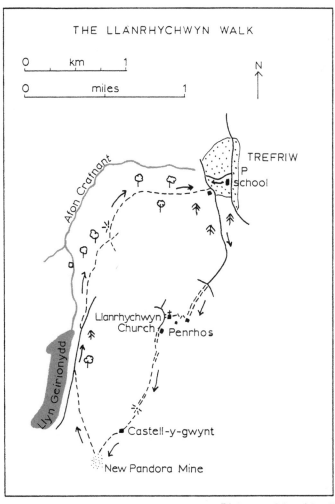

THE LLANRHYCHWYN WALK

0   km   1

0   miles   1

N

Afon Crafnant

TREFRIW

P

school

Llanrhychwyn
Church

Penrhos

Llyn Geirionydd

Castell-y-gwynt

New Pandora Mine

Distance: 8 km / 5 miles

DIRECTIONS: **From Trefriw to Llanrhychwyn:** From the car park (opposite the woollen mill) turn left onto the main road. Turn to the right up the steep road which borders the village school. As you climb up the slope, the road bears left passing Bryn Ysgol. Keep to the road

109

signed Llanrhychwyn (ignoring a road joining from the left) and continue to a T-junction. Turn left to follow the road which climbs the steep valley side for about one kilometre, with views over Nant Conwy towards Llanrwst. The road is quiet in winter but be aware of summer traffic.

The road levels out before reaching a crossroads (1.5 kilometres from Trefriw). Continue straight ahead to follow a track with a footpath sign for 400 metres to Tan-yr-eglwys. Follow the footpath sign passing to the right of the house. Immediately past their garden on the right, turn right up the steps and through the signed wooden gate. Steps lead up to a kissing gate beyond.

The path veers to the left passing a white cottage at a kissing gate. There is now a clear view of Llanrhychwyn church on the skyline ahead, sheltered by ancient yews. Look for the kissing gate to the right of the church. Beyond it turn left to the lych gate which still has the original door. The church is currently kept open.

LLANRHYCHWYN CHURCH

Llanrhychwyn Church was founded by a Celtic saint, St Rhychwyn in the 6th century. As you enter the building through the narrow, thick-walled 12th century doorway you are in the oldest corner of the building. An extra aisle to the north was added in the 16th century. It is known as Llywelyn's Church for Llywelyn Fawr (the Great) worshipped here. It is said that he built the church in Trefriw to save his wife, Joan, the climb you have just made. The 12th century font is thought to be the oldest in Wales and there are remnants of mediaeval glass. St Rhychwyn looks on from the window near the pulpit. Services are held at Christmas and on the 4th Sunday in June, August and September at 2pm.

Over Pen-y-drum to Llyn Geirionydd: Return to the lych gate and turn left to the metal kissing gate. Go straight ahead along the tarmac road which deteriorates to a track. Continue on the old track beyond Penrhos through two gates to a stile. Beyond it, turn left and, after 10 metres, turn right (signed) over rough ground. Continue up to a stile.

Exit from the track over the stile into featureless open ground. Head for a dip in the skyline straight ahead, following the grassy path in a shallow valley for 400 metres to a gate and stile. After crossing the stile, bear right to the ruins of a cottage by the old slate wall. Leaving the ruin to your right, follow the wall to its end. As you follow it the mountains will rise to meet you.

Where the stone wall ends abruptly, continue in the same direction down the slope heading towards the lake in the distance. As you descend, the chimney pots of Castell-y-Gwynt will come into view.

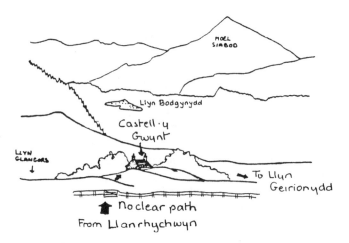

MOEL SIMBOD

Llyn Bodgynydd

Castell·y Gwynt

LLYN GLANGORS ↓

To Llyn Geirionydd

↑ No clear path

From Llanrhychwyn

Continue downhill towards the house through a metal gate rejoining the old track. Pass through the front yard of Castell-y-Gwynt, via stiles, to continue along the track which leads to the disused New Pandora Mine.

At a concrete building turn right across the mine tips through a gap in the first fence to find a stile on the boundary fence beyond. Cross the stile to follow a clear path through rough pasture descending the hill at an angle to join a gated road following the lakeshore. Turn right to the end of the lake.

The return to Trefriw: When you reach the end of the lake, leave the road to follow a path which runs between the road and a fence (keep the stream from Llyn Geirionydd on your left). There are two stiles on this level track which heads into the Crafnant Valley.

> *The dark holes of mine adits can be seen to the left of the stream. In the last century this was a busy industrial scene. A tramway led along this track bringing lead and zinc ores from the New Pandora Mine to a processing plant, in the Crafnant Valley below.*

Follow the track which now dwindles to a path to cross a small wooded gully. Pass through a wooden gate, continuing along the hillside with woodlands of dwarf oak, birch and hawthorn on the down slope side and a field wall on the right.

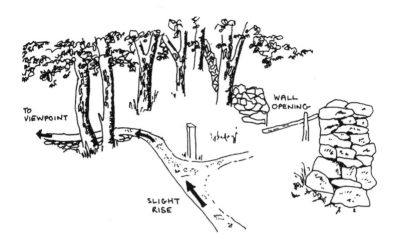

At a gap in the wall on the right there is a junction of paths; keep to the lower path which continues at the same level for about 100 metres to a viewpoint. From this rocky knoll there is a good view into the Crafnant Valley (see page 99).

The path descends gently for 1.5 kilometres leading across the steep, smooth hill slope of the Crafnant Valley. It passes through a small coniferous plantation before meeting the road of your outward journey. Turn left for 100 metres and then right to return down slope to Trefriw.